5 1/2 MENTORS

5 ½

MENTORS

HOW TO LEARN, GROW, AND DEVELOP FROM EVERYONE AND EVERYTHING

DOUG STEWART

LIONCREST
PUBLISHING

5 1/2 MENTORS
How to Learn, Grow, and Develop from Everyone and Everything

ISBN   978-1-5445-1722-3 *Hardcover*

      978-1-5445-1720-9 *Paperback*

      978-1-5445-1721-6 *Ebook*

      978-1-5445-1723-0 *Audiobook*

To my wife, Merideth – If I only have one life, I give it to you.

To my children, Kendall & Kendrick – If I could
only be one thing, I'd choose to be your dad.

To anyone who has ever felt misunderstood. I get it.

All speling and gramitikal erorrs compliments of dyslexia :—)

CONTENTS

INTRODUCTION

"Action may not always bring happiness, but there is no happiness without action."

—BENJAMIN DISRAELI

This book will *not* change your life.

You might have read other books that promise exactly that. After reading them, you're told your life will *automagically* change, and your wildest dreams will come true. You'll become faster than a speeding bullet, more powerful than a locomotive, and leap tall buildings in a single bound. Many books promise extraordinary results. Few, if any, deliver.

I assure you that you'll find no magic words or empty promises in these pages. If you're expecting instant gratification and transformation by reading this (or any other book, for that matter), you should put it down now. I guarantee you will be disappointed.

If you're looking for an honest, straightforward, and practical understanding of how to learn, grow, and develop from everyone and everything you encounter, this *is* the book for you.

As far as changing your life goes, there's only one thing capable of doing that, and it's not any book, film, religious experience, or anything else.

It's you.

INNATE GREATNESS

Innate greatness runs deep within all of us, and you are no different. All you have to do is draw it out. If you'd like a jump start on that, here's an exercise that may help.

Start by thinking of the most sentimental object you own. For me, it's a picture that my daughter drew when she was about four years old. It was a picture of a lake with a boat on it. In the picture, not only is she driving the boat, she's also pulling me on a wakeboard. This picture is one of those sentimental items that any proud father would hold near and dear to his heart. That's why it has hung on my office wall for the last five years. Every time I look at it, I smile.

This picture is made from the finest construction paper and crayons money can buy. When combined with the twenty-dollar frame I put around it, the total monetary value is slightly under twenty-one dollars.

Nonetheless, if someone offered me fifty dollars for that picture, I wouldn't sell it. One hundred dollars. Still wouldn't sell it. $500? No sale. If I'm being completely honest, there *is* a price where I would sell the picture. I'm not Mother Teresa. If you'd like to make an offer for more than $5,000, let's talk.

Chances are you own something of similar sentimental value. What is that priceless item for you? It might be your grandmother's wedding ring, a childhood toy, or a favorite book. It could be something that reminds you of a special time in your life.

You and that item have much more in common than you realize. First, there's nothing exactly like that item, and there is no other person exactly like you. Also, that item is worth the precise value you put on it, and the same is true for you. In the same way that the picture my daughter drew is worth much more to me than the twenty-one dollars it cost to make, your body, mind, spirit, and soul are infinitely valuable. Once you accept and activate that knowledge, your heart and mind will open to your true potential and purpose. The choice is yours to feel empowered by viewing yourself as the priceless, one-of-a-kind item you are, or the twenty-one-dollar collection of parts that's not worth anything to anyone. An effective way to begin to know how valuable you really are is to understand the distinction between confidence and courage.

Courage is something you can choose. Confidence is something you have to earn; it is the result of courage.

You can know everything there is to know about hitting a baseball, but until you gain the courage to step up to the plate, be willing to fail, and improve over time, you will never earn the right to be confident about hitting a baseball. The same is true with everything else in life.

Sometimes, it's not an issue of confidence or courage.

Rather, we believe we need permission to pursue our purpose, our passion, and who we were truly meant to be. If you feel like you need permission, here's a permission slip for you.

> By the power vested in me from the divine creator of the universe, I, Doug Stewart, officially give _____ full permission to pursue your passions and to accept yourself as the innately great and priceless person you are.

> From this day forward, you will double down on your strengths, forgive your weaknesses, and continue to see every victory as an opportunity for gratitude and every failure as an opportunity for wisdom.

Now that that's out of the way, let's move on to something else you don't need—motivation.

MOTIVATION IS WORTHLESS

Some people think of motivation as a prerequisite to taking action; it's not.

Think of motivation as the way you feel at 5:00 p.m. when you think about working out at 5:00 a.m....tomorrow. When the alarm goes off the next morning, motivation is usually nowhere to be found. Hit the snooze as much as you want; the motivation won't be there at 5:10, 5:20, or 5:30, either.

Motivation is a by-product of discipline. If you're disciplined enough to get out of bed when the alarm goes off, motivation will show up about ten minutes into the workout. It acts the same way with healthy eating. It's never there for that first bite of salad at dinnertime. Motivation appears later on, when you start feeling better from choosing healthier foods for several days in a row. Discipline comes first; motivation is what happens after you're disciplined enough to take action.

Another key distinction about motivation is that it's much more appealing when it includes something fun, which almost never offers any long-term benefit. How often does fun mean thirty minutes on the treadmill instead of watching a marathon of your favorite TV show? Ice cream always tastes better than kale, and procrastination is always more convenient than discipline.

You wouldn't feed garbage to a champion racehorse...all the time. It's okay to give a treat to a thoroughbred once in a while; just don't overindulge it. The same goes for your own self-care. Treat yourself like the champion you are. Allow yourself the occasional indulgence; just remember to consistently do the things your future self will benefit from the most.

Like purpose showing up after passionately pursuing something.

SELF-CARE

It's easy to replace self-care with escapism. Self-care is doing the things that prepare and allow us to be the healthiest version of ourselves—physically, mentally, and spiritually. Escapism is the act of doing things that provide a break from the reality of our daily routine. Allow yourself the occasional escape the same way you allow yourself the occasional tasty indulgence.

The eighty/twenty rule is a good way to manage your self-care. This means you dedicate 80 percent of your self-care time to perennial tasks that you'll thank yourself for doing in ten years. Perennial tasks are things like budgeting, planning meals for the week, going to therapy, and blocking time to call your loved ones. Likewise, you spend 20 percent of your time on activities that provide some form of escapism. This is the time you allocate to massages, pedicures, partying with friends, going out to dinner, retail therapy, binging on Netflix, and other fun things.

ALARM CLOCK MOMENT

Of course, I have no idea why you actually picked up this book. If it's because you feel like you're stuck in a personal or professional rut (or both) and are looking for a way to break out of it, I get it. I still get stuck. The same is true for everyone else as well (if they're willing to be honest with themselves).

We're all susceptible to falling into negative beliefs and patterns. Fear of loss or of failure, trauma, intellectual laziness, spiritual apathy, self-centeredness, bad advice, and ingrained philosophy learned from childhood are examples of how this happens. Many others exist, I'm sure. The key is figuring out how to get unstuck.

When I felt the most stuck in my life, someone came along who was willing to disrupt the negative pattern in which I was trapped. I'm grateful for this disruption in my life, because it helped me to realize that I was operating from the self-destructive way of seeing myself and the world.

I was believing and behaving like a victim, which was preventing me from gaining any sort of positive momentum. Until then, I wasn't accepting any responsibility for the outcomes in my life. That person challenged and encouraged me to me to wake up and realize that my *personal* development was my *personal* responsibility, rather than continuing to believe I was a victim of my circumstances. I call that my "alarm clock moment," which I'll talk more about in the next chapter. What are you waiting for to move forward? Permission? Access? To win the lottery?

You don't need any of those things to take control of and effect change in your life. Instead of waiting for something to happen that may never materialize, accept your innate greatness to take action, reach your full potential, and get the most out of your time on earth.

Don't waste time. Life isn't a storybook where everyone gets a fair chance. The good news is that you have *a* chance. The bad news is that that chance could be quite different based on some advantages or disadvantages. Unfortunately, things beyond your control will affect your chances of success. For me, it was my learning disabilities and victim thinking. Instead of worrying about them, let's accept them and take action to improve upon your circumstances. Some of those predetermining factors include income level, the neighborhood you grow up in, race, religion, educational background, gender, and many more.

Some people are shooting layups in life while others are shooting hook shots from half court. Both groups of people get a shot. Undoubtedly, one group has a much easier likelihood for success than the other.

Does everyone get a chance?

Yes.

Are the probabilities for success much different?

Absolutely.

Never forget that you *are* on the court and have a shot. Regardless of whether it's a layup or half-court hook shoot, take it! Shoot your shot. If the odds seem so insurmountably stacked against you, stack the deck in your favor or play a different game. Don't allow a disadvantage to stop you from shooting your shot.

Everyone gets stuck from time to time. Michael Jordan went into shooting slumps. Adele produced no music for several years. Elon Musk and everyone else you might think of as infallible have been stuck numerous times in their lives. They never stayed that way. Michael Jordan kept shooting, Adele kept singing, and Elon Musk kept innovating. The only people who stay stuck are the ones who don't act.

No matter how many shots you've missed, or even if you're stuck shooting past half-court all the way from the opponent's free-throw line, shoot your shot. Sometimes, the only way to get unstuck is to keep shooting.

THE SPIDER AND THE WASP

If you're having difficulty choosing courage to get unstuck, it might help to understand the healthy boundary that exists between reality and perception. This idea became clear to me a few years ago when I was doing yard work and got bitten by a spider. The bite hurt for about fifteen minutes.

After I put anti-itch ointment on it, the pain subsided, and I never thought about it again.

Later that same day, I was cutting the grass while a wasp buzzed around the yard. No matter where I went, the wasp followed, menacing me like a tiny, flying stalker. Its presence caused me to obsess over the idea that the wasp *could* sting me at any given moment, and that's not where my anxiety ended. My fear then went to work on my creativity, which resulted in a diabolical story that seemed all too real at the time. I thought...

The wasp is going to sting me and cause excruciating pain. My face will swell up like a balloon, and my throat will start to close. When it becomes difficult to breathe, my wife will call an ambulance. If I survive the ride, I'll arrive at the hospital, where they'll do some unspeakably uncomfortable procedure. If I survive that, I'll receive a totally unaffordable medical bill in a few weeks, which will plunge me into financial hardship. From there, I'll miss mortgage payments, and the bank will foreclose on my house. At that point, my family will be homeless, which will cause my wife to take the kids and leave me. When I lose them, I'll spiral into a deep depression, become completely detached from society, and develop a serious drug problem. That will put me back in the hospital. Damn it! More medical bills. After that, I'll lose my *ever-loving* mind and get admitted into a psychiatric institution, where I'll spontaneously yell

"Hakuna Matata!" all day for the next thirty years, until I die of loneliness, wearing a snug-fitting white jacket in a cold, dark, padded room...

All because of a wasp that never actually stung me. Choosing to live in a reality that doesn't yet exist is hell on earth.

I wish I could say that chain of events is nothing more than a creative writing exercise; it's not. My fear uses my creativity against me. Has your fear ever turned your creativity against you like that? If so, that's okay because fear isn't necessarily a bad thing. When it's used correctly, fear keeps you safe.

A few thousand years ago, our ancestors were walking through a jungle or forest. If they heard a rustling in the bushes, their fear spoke to them. "That might be something that could eat me. I'll keep my eyes open and my hands ready to use my club." If our ancestors had no fear, they might have responded a little differently. [Insert Olaf voice] "Ooh, I bet that's a butterfly! I think I'll go take a look. Hi, butterfly!" Then, of course, there would be a few loud snarls and screams, followed by the crunching of bones, and those particular ancestors would be eaten. Survival of the fittest involves *some* level of fear.

It was right for me to notice the wasp and take precautions to not get stung. I kept my eyes on it and tried to work away from it whenever possible. Where I went wrong was to allow my fear to continue telling me the story about a reality that was most likely *never* going to happen.

The story about the spider and the wasp can teach a valuable lesson, which is that the pain of reality is rarely as bad as the suffering induced by our imagination. As Mark Twain put it, "I am an old man who has seen a great many troubles. But most of them never happened."

In whatever way you feel stuck, this book will provide unique insight that will help you create ideas to take the type of action that will help *you* get *you* unstuck.

WHAT MENTORSHIP *REALLY* DOES

Until now, most people have thought of a mentor as an infallible guru who will

- **M**otivate you to do amazing things.
- **E**ncourage your growth.
- **N**udge you in the right direction.
- **T**ackle your toughest issues.
- **O**rganize your thoughts.
- **R**ealign your perspective.

Rarely, if ever, will a single mentor accomplish all of those things. On an exceptional day, a mentor might do one of them. If you run into someone who says they can do it all (usually for a small fee), run! That person is much more capable of *ruining* your life than *saving* it. As the ninth-century Buddhist monk Linji Yixuan put it, "If you meet the Buddha on the road, kill him."

As explicit as his words may sound, Linji was not calling for the murder of his beloved spiritual icon. He was pointing out that anybody claiming to be the Buddha is lying. Nobody will be your savior, and that includes mentors.

It's worth noting that this idea isn't exclusive to Buddhism; many religions have their way of saying the same thing.

The best mentors typically don't have time to save you; they're busy changing the world in their own innovative ways. If you've been hoping for someone to become your go-to for everything, don't beat yourself up. I waited a long time for a magic mentor to show up and save me, too. Sadly, as bad as I wanted to be a Jedi, my Yoda never showed up.

Mentors save the heavy lifting for you. Think of them as your spotter during a bench-press session at the gym. They don't lift the weight for you; they provide support.

Instead of encouraging you to pin your hopes on something (or someone) unrealistic, this book will tell you what mentorship *really* does. Opportunities to learn, grow, and

Yoda never showed up.

develop are abundant in life. All you must do is accept and activate your innate greatness to access mentorship from everyone and everything around you.

In this book, you will meet the 5 ½ mentors that have fundamentally changed the trajectory of my life. These mentors are also available to you if you're willing to do the work. I will dedicate one chapter to each of the following:

- The Anti-Mentor (Half-Mentor)
- The Micro-Mentor
- The Digital Mentor
- The Categorical Mentor
- The Mentor
- The World-View Mentor

Before we get there though, Chapter 1 will explain how, as a young person, I battled myriad learning disabilities including ADHD (Attention Deficit Hyperactivity Disorder), bipolar type II, narcolepsy, and severe dyslexia before someone disrupted my self-defeating pattern and helped me, along with the help and support from my mentors, to save myself. By reading my story, I hope you will realize that no matter how stuck you feel, you have everything you need to stop spinning your wheels, get out of the ditch, and move forward.

CHAPTER 1

—

THE VICTIM

"*I can say I'm mad and I hate everything, but nothing changes until I change myself.*"

–KENDRICK LAMAR

Have you ever felt stupid?

I don't mean have you ever done something or said anything stupid. We've all done those things. An example of *doing* something stupid is mistakenly copying the entire company on an email with a criticism of your boss in it. Better yet, it's showing up to an office party dressed as Little Bo Peep only to find out that it was *not* a costume party. I'm asking if you've ever felt like the core of your being is actually stupid. Let's consult with *Merriam-Webster* to make sure I'm clear on what I mean.

stu·pid | \ 'stü-pəd

1. Slow of mind
2. Given to unintelligent decisions or acts
3. Lacking intelligence or reason

Have you ever felt like that?

I have.

Not only have I *felt* that way, I have documentation that *I was born that way!*

When I was around eleven years old, I had fallen far behind the rest of my classmates. It was a trend that had begun a few years prior and had been getting steadily worse with each passing school year.

I had always been an impulsive child. If something didn't immediately occupy my mind, I would move onto something else, usually without thinking through my actions or their consequences. For example, I would fling a pencil at my friend's head across the room before my hands consulted with my brain about whether or not it was a good idea. Side note: it was *never* a good idea.

By the time I was eleven, my parents and teachers had enough of my disruptive and wild behavior and decided to find out what was wrong with me. My parents told me that I was selected to take a test (provided by the state of North Carolina) out of all the kids in my class because I was "special." I may have struggled academically, but the BS detector in my brain worked fine, so I knew that this notion of "special" was not the good kind.

The test lasted all day. I felt overwhelmed with the number of confusing questions and was glad when it was over. At some point, my parents and I expected to get a one-page summary of my test results. Instead, we received a packet filled with detailed reports outlining my disabilities and deficiencies.

The report revealed I had ADHD, and my reading comprehension was almost nonexistent. At eleven years old, I still couldn't write the alphabet. That was a big hint that I had much more going on than ADHD. Later on, not only was I diagnosed with everything I mentioned at the conclusion of the last chapter, but it was also revealed that I was struggling with sensory issues and speech impediments as well. Other than that, I was perfectly normal!

Although some might take comfort in these sorts of discoveries, they did nothing to help me at that point; all they did was label me and make me feel shame, fear, and guilt for my entire childhood.

The doctors prescribed Ritalin to help with my ADHD, but

it only made things worse in a lot of ways. The side effects (stomach pain, listlessness, loss of appetite, and an overall sense of haziness) were horrendous. I disliked them so much that I started hiding the pills to make my mom think I took them. That solution was not well thought out, because it made everyone think the medication wasn't having any effect, which resulted in prescriptions with higher dosages. Finally, my mom caught on to what I was doing and asked me why I was hiding the pills. I told her, "Mom, if this is what normal feels like, I don't want to be normal." After hearing that, she decided to stop medicating me.

Despite my struggles, there was one big ray of sunshine cast onto my challenging childhood. Lucky for me, I was born with height and athleticism.

HOOP DREAMS

At thirteen years old, I dunked a basketball for the first time in a game. Soon after, I began to separate myself from other players my age. Basketball became my passion. It was my escape from the inferiority that came with not measuring up academically.

As a ninth-grader, I was ranked as the fourth-best freshman basketball player in the state of North Carolina. This caught the attention of numerous Division I universities looking for scholarship athletes with the height, athleticism, and shooting ability I possessed. As a result, my mind began wandering to the bright lights of an NBA career. So what if I couldn't read well or stay focused in class? I was going to have my name announced in front of tens of thousands of screaming fans someday...or so I figured.

My identity, as a young person, became a paradox. In one world, people cheered for me and told me I was special (the good kind this time). In another world, I was stupid. If you were in my shoes, in which world would you choose to live?

Basketball became my life. What other options did I have? From the time I took that test in elementary school to high school graduation, I never passed a grade on my own merit. My teachers passed me either because they couldn't bear the thought of my disrupting their classroom for another year or because they didn't want to stand in the way of my hoop dreams. Nobody wanted to be known as the teacher responsible for preventing a student from fulfilling a destiny with professional sports.

All I wanted to do was play Division I college basketball, hoping that it would be my ticket to the NBA. That way, I would never have to think about the identity where I felt so vastly inferior. Unfortunately, that dream was shattered in one fateful moment as a junior in high school.

I was selected to play in the Amateur Athletic Union tournament at the Wide World of Sports complex in Orlando, Florida. The best young players in the country gather at this annual event to showcase their skills for top-ranked colleges, NBA scouts, and anyone else with a stake in youth basketball.

Before playing a game, I watched a team from Florida during its warm-ups. That's where I saw a young man named Amar'e Stoudemire for the first time.

Amar'e was six feet eleven. He could run like a point guard, jump out of the gym, and seemed strong enough to bench press the team bus—with everyone in it, including the mascot. I first witnessed his dominance when he exploded toward the hoop during a lay-up drill. He launched himself off the ground like a SpaceX rocket, passed the ball through his legs from one hand to the other—midair—and dunked the ball with the force of a titanium sledgehammer. His athletic ability was off the charts, and I thought to myself, "If that's what the NBA looks like, I am *not* going to be in it."

Despair washed over me, as everything I had banked my life's purpose on was shattered. It seemed like I had invested my basketball life with Bernie Madoff. Much like his financial clients, I was left speechless and depleted of my most valuable resources.

Unfortunately, I did not have an acceptable alternative, so

I lowered my expectations. I figured I could still play ball in college, and instead of getting dismantled by Amar'e in the NBA, I might be able to play professionally overseas.

After that tournament, Division I colleges still wanted to talk to me. After all, kids like Amar'e aren't all that common, so the college coaches still needed to bring in players at the next, somewhat more *human* level of athleticism.

> At the time, the best high school players could go straight to the NBA, and that's exactly what Amar'e did. He opted to enter the 2002 NBA Draft, where the Phoenix Suns selected him with the ninth overall pick. It seems unfathomable to me that eight other players were thought to be better than him that year.
>
> Amar'e won Rookie of the Year and went on to play in six NBA All-Star games. After watching him, it's safe to say, that's six more than I would have played in.

Unfortunately, my interactions with those high-profile basketball schools always ended like a bad first date. The coach would approach me after one of my games and say something like, "Hey, great game, Doug. We love watching you play. Send us a copy of your transcripts so we can talk about scheduling an official visit with you." Like a bad first date that leaves you waiting by the phone without a callback, once I sent my transcripts, I never heard from them again.

LIFE, LIBERTY, AND THE PURSUIT OF A 1.8 GPA

Liberty University in Lynchburg, Virginia, was the only

school with a Division I basketball program that gave me a chance. I don't know why they were willing to overlook my less than stellar academic performance; I also didn't question it. Instead, I happily agreed to attend there in the fall on a basketball scholarship.

When I got there, I learned about the NCAA Eligibility Center. That's the governing body of the NCAA that ensures the student athletes meet its standards for academic excellence. How does the NCAA define academic excellence? It calls it a GPA of 1.8; not exactly the qualifications of a Rhoades scholar, is it?

The Clearing House took one look at my high school transcripts, and even though I was already enrolled at Liberty, it determined that my grades were insufficient to be a high school graduate. As a result, I had to redshirt my freshman year, because I was essentially suspended from playing basketball until I met the academic requirements.

> To redshirt in a freshman year means to withdraw from participating in a sport to extend the period of playing eligibility for another year.

Before I would be cleared to play, I had to earn my first GPA.

The results of that first semester were not good. I received a whopping 1.4 GPA, which was far short of the prestigious standard of 1.8 to which the NCAA holds its student athletes accountable. Soon after, someone from the school informed me that I would lose my scholarship unless my 1.4 became a 1.8. They also told me that I was required to report to my academic advisor, Sarah Baker, for further instruction.

I decided to get this over with and made my way to Sarah's office. Before I got one foot in the door, she pointed at me and said, "Doug Stewart, do you know what your problem is?"

At only nineteen years of age, I knew enough about life to understand that when someone poses a question like that, they're not waiting for an answer. They're framing their words as a question to create an awkward silence for a second or two. The purpose is to make you squirm before they say something about you that you do not yet know about you.

With visible frustration, Sarah continued, "You're a victim of your own thinking."

You might think that those words were insulting or hurtful to a young person; they weren't. Hearing them actually had the opposite effect; they gave me a sense of relief.

Never before had an adult, educator, or leader of any kind

said out loud what I had believed about myself, which was that I was a victim. I felt that way because I didn't ask for all those disabilities. In my mind, it wasn't my fault that I couldn't keep up with the other kids in class. "Blame someone else," I always thought. "I didn't ask for any of these disabilities; it's not my fault."

Sarah's speech had a big impact on me. I knew she wasn't angry because my grades were garbage; it was because she saw something in me that I couldn't see or wasn't willing to see. She knew that I was telling myself a false story.

Sarah wasn't done. Rather than state the problem and let me go, she said, "You'll come to my office every day until you change your mind. You will not be a victim any longer."

"Oh, that's cute," I thought to myself. "She has no idea who she's dealing with right now." Little did she know that while most kids were learning about geometry, literature, art, and science, I had developed my own skills. Think of it like the movie *Taken,* when Liam Neeson's character said, "What I do have are a very particular set of skills; skills I have acquired over a very long career; skills that make me a nightmare for people like you!" In this case, I had an outstanding ability to wear down teachers, take away their good intentions, and make them either cry or quit. Of course, Neeson was trying to save his daughter from kidnapping; I was hoping to continue making excuses and get out of doing schoolwork. Nonetheless, I was pretty dang great at it.

Teachers had given up on me my whole life. Who could blame them? I was a real pain. I assumed Sarah would last a few days. If she was especially resilient, she might endure my bad attitude for a couple of weeks. The best-case scenario, I thought, would have been if she could get me to a 1.8 GPA for the next semester. We could both move on with our lives.

A PICTURE IS WORTH...A COLLEGE BASKETBALL SCHOLARSHIP

I arrived at Sarah's office the next day, realizing that people can only be frustrated for so long before they explode like an egg that's been left in the microwave too long. If she was still running hot, this would have been a short endeavor. Instead, her energy was completely different. She was almost giddy with excitement, and it threw me off my game.

When I walked through the door, she didn't point at me this time. Instead, she greeted me with a smile and handed me a stack of construction paper and a box of crayons. "Every day," she told me, "we'll be drawing pictures together. At the beginning of each meeting, I will read your assignments, and you will draw pictures to complete them." She explained further that she didn't need to understand what I was drawing, as long as I did.

I'd like you to pause for a moment so you can fully appreciate the image of a completely humbled and mostly perplexed six foot seven and 230-pound college basketball player, coloring with crayons in the office of his academic advisor. My friends and teammates enjoyed that image quite a bit whenever they walked by her office and saw me with a crayon in hand. All I needed to complete the absurd visual was to place my Transformers backpack into one of those kindergarten cubbies in the corner of her office.

Sarah gave me permission to learn things differently. Albert Einstein said it best: "Everyone is a genius. But if you judge a fish by its ability to climb a tree, it will live its whole life believing that it is stupid."

My form of dyslexia manifests as a disconnect between my brain and my fingertip; it has nothing to do with my speech. There's also an associated vision problem, where I read words backward and sometimes I see words that aren't there. So you might imagine how much of an undertaking it was for me to write this book.

People think in pictures, so she knew if I couldn't see the word, she could help me see the picture. From there, I could draw the answer.

Going forward with my classes, it wasn't like I got special treatment. I didn't take any tests verbally, for example, nor did I get more time to complete assignments. The only thing that changed was that Sarah encouraged me to learn *my way* instead of force-feeding me the generally accepted teaching methods that worked well for other students.

Sarah instructed me to quit playing a game I couldn't win. Instead, she encouraged me to change the rules of engagement and play a game for which I was innately built. After all, Shaquille O' Neal wouldn't make a good racehorse jockey, so why force him (and the unfortunate horse) to compete in a game he can't win. Put a basketball in his hands and see what happens. It's naturally a much better fit.

We did this picture-drawing exercise every day for a couple of weeks, and some strange things started to happen. First, I showed up for class. Until that point, good attendance was not at the top of my priority list. By being present, I began to feel more comfortable asking the professors questions and interacting with others. I also started to turn assignments in on time. Rather than pulling a disappearing act on quiz and test days, I actually took them!

All these changes resulted from Sarah's seeing something more than the overprivileged, lazy, high-profile athlete who gets everything handed to him on a silver platter. She saw beyond the stereotype that even I believed in too much.

Throughout that semester, I never checked my grades. Academic performance had never revealed anything positive in my life before that, so I wasn't about to ruin this newfound confidence by seeing that I still wasn't performing up to par. What a bummer that would have been.

Finally, the moment of truth arrived. The semester was over, and most of the other kids had already gone home for break. I had to stick around and wait for the grades to be posted, because if that 1.4 GPA didn't rise to 1.8, I would need to pack up my dorm and move out permanently.

I was sitting in the school library when the grades were made available online. Reluctantly and with my eyes three-quarters closed, I clicked the button that said "view grades."

At that moment, I realized that Sarah was right. I had been a victim of my own thinking, and I was telling myself a story that was never true. My destiny would be whatever I decided it was going to be. My grades did not get to 1.8; they went to 3.4!

EYES WIDE OPEN

Suddenly, a potent cocktail of emotions swirled warm and lively throughout my veins. You would assume that I was overjoyed by this stunning achievement. I was not. Rather, I was terrified. Why? It proved how right Sarah was about me. I had been operating as a victim for my whole life. The responsibility for all those poor academic results was 100 percent mine. My eyes were open for the first time, and I had to own this realization. It was officially time for me to step in and live with a new mindset of accountability. This was my alarm clock moment. I had fallen incredibly far behind, and it would now be my life's mission to never let that happen again.

TURN INSIGHT INTO ACTION

Take a moment to consider the alarm clock moments in your life. Think about the special accomplishments you've had or challenging times you've faced. In what ways have these moments shaped you?

For more information about my alarm clock moment, check out my TEDx talk at www.dougstewart919.com.

Suddenly, I understood that I had much more potential than I thought. I didn't know specifically what that potential was yet. That didn't matter. What meant the most was that I was also going to live my potential with zero attachment to timing or achievement. The results didn't matter nearly as much as the journey. With this realization, I was now free to enjoy the abundance of opportunities in life to learn, grow, and develop.

Once I realized that my potential was greater than I previously imagined, I embarked on a quest for knowledge, and I wasn't going to restrict myself to only what I could learn in school. I read books by Seth Godin, Napoleon Hill, Robert Kiyosake, Dale Carnegie, and Zig Ziglar. These writings were excellent sources to develop my potential.

To be honest, I didn't maintain that 3.4 throughout my college career. I finished college with an acceptable GPA of 2.8, which was still double the 1.4 with which I started.

Soon after my alarm clock moment, other internal realizations swept over me. My eyes were wide open for the first time in my life. I began to realize that I was also deficient emotionally, spiritually, and relationally. By unraveling all these areas of need, I sought mentorship as an avenue to achieve what I wanted in life—contentment, fulfillment, and purpose.

I'm forever grateful for the way Sarah was willing to disrupt my pattern and point me in the right direction. By my junior year, she had taken another job. Meanwhile, I was searching for someone else to help me. The problem was that the mentors I wanted were unavailable; they were busy doing their own things and unwilling to give me the time of day.

Undeterred, I used my recent shift in mindset to uncover mentorship in new ways. That is how I began to form my thoughts on the 5½ mentors. It's what helped me to go from that alarm clock moment to where I am today.

As a keynote speaker, Dale Carnegie–certified instructor,

and coach of many business leaders, I get paid to do some of the things that used to land me in detention. I get people energized and encourage them to take action. Today, I feel privileged to help all those kids in school—who I couldn't keep up with academically—to communicate better, improve their relationships, and form creative business solutions.

In high school, nobody thought that I would someday be working with and coaching CEOs of major companies, innovative entrepreneurs, and tenured professors, among others. I get to help the people I once envied—proof positive that if we're willing to do the work and have the right mindset, we can achieve things we never thought possible.

In the next chapter, I'll share how my daughter, as a four-year-old, epitomized the attitude and actions that attract the best mentors. The story explains how she unknowingly used the idea of mentorship to accomplish a goal. If you embody her approach from that situation, you will undoubtedly accomplish more than you could ever imagine. When it comes to fear, shame, or anything holding you back, it's time to *let it go!*

CHAPTER 2

———

THE MINDSET

"You were born with wings; why prefer to crawl through life?"

—RUMI

When my daughter was four years old, she provided me with the perfect example of what it means to have the mentorship mindset.

One day, my sweet, blonde baby girl looked up at me with hands on her hips and said, "Daddy, take me skating."

As her dad, this was interesting because I knew a few major obstacles stood in her way:

1. She did *not* own a pair of skates.
2. She had *never* before been skating.
3. She did *not* know how to skate.

"Sweetheart, do you know how to skate?" I asked. As a coach, I knew the only way to uncover the catalyst for Kendall's demand was to ask questions. I needed to know the facts before I could address the situation.

"Yes!" Kendall responded emphatically.

I stepped back for a moment and smiled. "How do you know how to skate?"

Without missing a beat, my daughter answered, "Fah-rozen!"

Something in the Disney movie *Frozen* made my daughter believe she knew how to skate. I was making progress in my investigation yet missing a key piece of information. I should have asked her one more question: "sweetheart, can you tell me how Fah-rozen taught you to skate?" Because of my haste in getting to the heart of the situation, I had to watch one hour and forty-eight minutes of the movie to get to the part that made Kendall believe she could skate.

In case you're not familiar with the movie, it takes place in the fictional kingdom of Arendelle, where two sisters, Elsa and Anna, inherit the ruling authority over a bustling citizenship. One of the key plot points is that Elsa has magical powers that allow her to turn everything into ice.

Frozen follows the typical Disney movie sequence of events, where things start off great and somehow go tragically bad before, eventually, good triumphs over evil and everyone lives happily ever after.

In this case, the last (happily ever after) scene features a kingdom-wide celebration, where Elsa uses her powers to give everyone skates made of actual ice and turns the kingdom's courtyard into an ice-skating rink. Suddenly, everybody in the kingdom *automagically* becomes an Olympic-level skater.

That scene must have told my daughter that only two things stood between her and performing breathtaking triple axels: ice and a pair of skates.

I decided to let her see what she could do and took her skating the next day. When we got to the rink, I sat her up on the counter to put tiny starter skates on her tiny feet. Then, I carried her out to the center of the rink, placed her down, removed my hands, took one step back, and...thump! Her bottom immediately hit the ice. At that exact moment, Kendall looked up at me and said, "Daddy, my skates are broken!"

"Baby, your skates aren't broken," I explained. "You don't know how to skate."

The life lesson worked well. She then allowed me to teach her how to skate. About ten minutes later, Kendall was able to stand on her skates without falling. We would have to work on the triple axels and double toe-loops next time.

As soon as she got comfortable standing, the DJ made an announcement: "Everybody clear the rink. It's time to race! First, the boys; then the girls. Everybody else, please get your butts off the ice."

Much like my wife, Kendall is fiercely competitive. Once she heard that a race was happening, she wanted in!

"Daddy, I want to race!"

"I'm sorry, sweetheart. You can't race because you still can't skate."

I carried her off the ice and thought to myself, "Once she watches the boys' race, she'll realize she's not yet at that skill level. Her desire to race will be a nonfactor after that."

About five minutes later, the boys lined up, and the DJ began the countdown. "Everybody on your mark, get set, go!"

As the boys raced around the rink, I took careful notice of Kendall's reaction. She was not overly impressed. In fact, she looked more confident than ever!

After the boys' race was over, the DJ announced that it was time for the girls to line up. Kendall pleaded with me, "Daddy, I *really* want to race. Please, can I race? Please!"

I figured this might have been a good opportunity for a second life lesson. So I said, "Baby, if you can make it to the starting line, go for it." That's when Kendall looked up at me in a way that only a daughter can look at her father and said, "Can you come with me? I'm scared." With my heart melted into a puddle of unconditional love, I did what any self-respecting dad would have done in that situation. I gave in.

As the other girls were making their way to the starting line,

I scooped up my little four-year-old competitor and made our way onto the ice. When we got in position, I put her down and saw how incredibly proud of herself she was for being able to stand there without falling.

I looked to our right and then to the left. There were no other cute, little, blonde four-year-old girls at the starting line. The girls all around us weren't just older girls; they looked like they played professional roller derby. In comparison to my pixie of a four-year-old daughter, they looked like the Monstars basketball team in the movie *Space Jam*. They were actually super sweet, average-sized girls. It was only in comparison to Kendall—who was so little at the time—that they looked much bigger.

A strong sense of guilt began to wash over me as I envisioned my little girl getting shoulder-blocked into the walls of the rink. I pictured it looking like one of the Monstars in *Space Jam* obliterating Tweety Bird while going for a loose ball. Sure, her confidence would be crushed. More importantly, so would her tiny body.

Parents are always worrying about their children getting hurt, physically or emotionally. In that way, this situation was my worst nightmare. I looked down at my daughter to see if there was one more chance that she would let me whisk her away to the safety of a plastic chair and a hot cocoa from the concession stand.

No chance; there was nothing but courage and determination in her eyes. She was laser focused and crouched into an athletic stance. Her steely eyed glare was reminiscent of Michael Jordan staring down the game-winning shot with time about to expire. There was no way she was going to leave the rink without racing or at least falling several thousand times before her butt skidded across the finish line.

After a few moments of nervous tension and sweaty anticipation (from me), the DJ got back on the loudspeaker. "Ladies, on your mark, get set, go!"

On his signal, the roller derby girls took off like they were shot out of a cartoon cannon. The race was on. As everybody flew past her, Kendall looked back at me and screamed, "Daddy, push me *really fast!*"

She got back in her athletic stance, and I guided her around the rink as best as I could, holding onto her hips and trying to not let her fall...too often. It was a lot like running a three-legged race when you take a step or two forward, fall down, take another step, fall down, again, and again, and again. Your best hope is to learn how to not land on your face *every* time.

If this were a Disney movie, Elsa would have shown up and pointed at Kendall, and my little girl would have left a blue flame of ice-powered rocket fuel behind her as she whizzed past the competition. Sadly, life is not a Disney movie. Instead, I'm pretty sure we got lapped five times in a three-lap race. Maybe it just seemed that way.

Finally, we got to the final turn, and I realized that the race had been over for several minutes. I heard wild cheering, looked up, and saw that everyone in the rink was at the finish line encouraging Kendall to cross. The scene was like a real-life version of the final moments in *Frozen*, when everyone is in the courtyard celebrating Anna and Elsa's triumph over the evil prince. Somehow, Kendall's will to succeed and sheer determination caused a recreation of the exact conditions she was hoping to achieve that day.

When we crossed, the entire rink burst into applause. It was a surreal moment that put a big smile on my daughter's face. It was worth every second of nervousness or fear I had at the beginning of our journey that day. As unlikely as her goal seemed when she first presented it to me, she had enough influence over the situation to make it work.

INFLUENCE VERSUS AUTHORITY

That moment of accomplishment for my daughter gave me a crystal-clear vision of the mindset required to attract the best mentors in life. Kendall used her mindset on herself to influence me to activate my authority. That allowed her to accomplish something she couldn't have done by herself. Meanwhile, I had the experience of using my authority (support) to be a part of something positive that I would never have chosen to do otherwise.

I didn't give Kendall any special access or privilege. We didn't need to travel to the magical world of Arendelle, either. Kendall's attitude, drive, and enthusiasm compelled me, as a mentor, to help her accomplish her goal. No magical ice powers were necessary.

A SUPPLEMENT, NOT A CURE

This story also drives home the idea that mentors aren't the most essential part of success in life; they're a supplement. Much like taking all the vitamins in the world won't help if you eat garbage all the time, mentorship only helps after three prerequisites are met.

 You must already be doing the work.
 You need to be assertive toward achieving your goal.
 You also need to be willing to make mistakes. Not only

that, you *must* make mistakes. A mentor once told me, "If you're not moving around enough to knock something over every once in a while, you're not moving around enough."

COMFORT ZONES

The idea of making mistakes speaks to a popular misconception about the need to constantly "step outside of your comfort zone." Countless clichés exist around how growth and success *only* happen from the mysterious space that lies *outside* your comfort zone. In reality, that's not the most accurate advice.

Comfort zones are *not* a bad thing. In fact, they're the *most important* place for you to be. The comfort zone is like sleeping in your own bed at night. Your bed provides a place for necessary rest, rejuvenation, and safety.

If you stayed awake for five consecutive days, your body and mind would surely break down. You would become emotionally broken, your relationships would deteriorate, your performance at work would suffer, and your physical health would be in serious jeopardy. All those things would happen as a result of constantly being outside of your comfort zone (your bed). If you get too far outside of your comfort zone, that's called trauma. When you're so far removed from where you're comfortable, it can be difficult to emotionally recover.

Operating exclusively from your comfort zone isn't a good thing either, because real growth is impossible if you don't experience new things and take on new challenges.

The sweet spot is where you commonly wander about six feet outside of your comfort zone. You can still see it and even touch it (if you wanted to). By operating from a safe distance, you'll avoid trauma and eventually expand your comfort zone. Then, you can stray another six feet away and try that on for size. This way, you consistently gain more space in which to operate comfortably.

GETTING STARTED

Mentorship doesn't help us get started. Once we're already doing the work, it helps us to continue the momentum we've established. This point is made from a scene in a popular Netflix show called *The Ranch*. In that scene, Ashton Kutcher's character, Colt Bennett, is sitting on the porch with his brother, Rooster.

Colt walks onto the porch and says, "Hey, man, is it okay if we don't talk tonight and just get drunk?" His brother smiles and responds, "I can't *get* drunk with you, but I can *maintain being* drunk with you." In this case, once Colt does the work of getting drunk, his brother will help him to stay that way. My hope is that we leverage the mentorship in our lives for somewhat more beneficial reasons. Nonetheless, I believe my point is still made.

Mentors are never by our side at the starting line. They're at a checkpoint a little further down the race. Another way to think of it is to say that there are no water tables at the start of a marathon. Good news is that there's always beer at the finish line!

Now that you know that the role of mentors in your life isn't to get you started, the next chapter will tell you everything you need to know about the exact amount of responsibility they have for the outcomes in your personal development journey.

CHAPTER 3

RESPONSIBILITY

Below you will find an exhaustive list of any and all the roles and responsibilities that others have on your mindset, attitude, actions, and results on your overall development.

CHAPTER 4

THE ANTI-MENTOR

"You have heard that it was said, 'Love your neighbor and hate your enemy.' But I tell you, love your enemies too."

—MATTHEW 5:43-44

Now that we've established that your *personal* development is 100 percent your *personal* responsibility, let's talk about the first of the 5½ mentors.

Chaos creators, sandpaper people, and Haterade drinkers—they're all aliases for the anti-mentors in our lives. Anti-mentors are enough to make the Pope cuss and a Happy Meal frown. Even Mr. Rogers doesn't want them in his neighborhood. Extraordinary poet and playwright Oscar Wilde may have provided the most accurate depiction of the anti-mentor when he said, "Some cause happiness *wherever* they go; others *whenever* they go."

When you first saw the cover of this book, you may have wondered what I meant by a half-mentor. Perhaps you thought, "Why 5 ½ mentors and not six or five?" The reason is that your natural inclination is likely to avoid *any* interactions with someone so seemingly negative, figuring the less you have to deal with them, the better off you are.

While I understand the wisdom behind that thinking, in reality, they're one of the most valuable assets we have to our personal growth and development. Due to this struggle between an involuntary aversion to anti-mentors and the supreme value we can extract from them by reframing their role in our lives, I believe they're appropriately deemed the status of half-mentor.

To draw value from anti-mentors, we must understand the many valuable learning opportunities they provide. It's easy to demonize these types of people, but there's a better way to interact with them. Think about some of the following ways to reframe the role of various anti-mentors in your life.

- People who annoy you teach you patience.
- People who anger you teach you forgiveness.
- People who abandon you teach you resilience.
- People who question you teach you how to think.
- People who irritate you the most can be your greatest teachers...

...if you let them. Anti-mentors help you to uncover your blind spots. They help you understand things you wouldn't figure out by only being around people who agree with you all the time.

TURN INSIGHT INTO ACTION

Think about the anti-mentors in your life. Surely, at least one or two exist. Some of us have many; others are so fearful of catching their negativity, they steer completely clear of them.

Ask yourself, would you rather view people who are different as adversaries or as allies to your growth?

Opportunities to have more productive interactions with anti-mentors are everywhere. Someone could have something potentially enlightening for us to experience that we see as nothing more than discomfort. Oftentimes, growth is disguised as discomfort.

Of course, anti-mentors can also take shape as the coworker who chews too loudly in the break room. They could be the family member that talks ad nauseum about ridiculous conspiracy theories at family gatherings. Another example could be the neighbor that lets their dog poop in your yard and never picks it up. Maybe some of your anti-mentors are much worse; they could be people who have seriously wronged you, hurt you, or abandoned you.

We have to be careful to protect our energy from the most

dubious examples of anti-mentors. Nonetheless, don't be so quick to run away and forfeit meaningful opportunities to learn, grow, and develop from all of them.

I'm willing to bet you can recall a previous encounter with a similar personality—someone from your past who had a knack for bringing out the worst in you. Perhaps in recalling such an encounter, you admittedly got angry or even bitter, and then avoided that person, learning nothing from the experience. If that's the case, don't worry. Now is your chance to embrace new perspective and make up for the lesson you missed.

Rather than avoiding your annoying coworker (or whoever this person may be), try observing them with a touch of curiosity. Watch what specifically annoys you, and ask yourself, "Why does this bother me so much? What if I just let it go?" and "What can I learn from this person?"

If you realize that people who talk too loudly on the phone annoy you *a lot*, remember that when *you* make phone calls. If mispronouncing your name is a particular irritant for you, make it a point to focus on someone's name every time they introduce themselves. In addition to potentially improving your relationship skills, you will develop better forgiveness, patience, compassion, empathy, and understanding.

Incarnations of the anti-mentor will challenge you for your

entire life. It's important to realize that they're not always wrong. Sometimes, you're wrong. You're human, which means you have faults and you (like everyone else) will be wrong from time to time.

Other times, there is no right or wrong, just *different*. It's easy to become annoyed or defensive when people disagree with us. Be willing to listen and seek to understand those who are different and view things from an opposing viewpoint. That will break down blind spots and allow us to discover more truth in our lives.

EVIL OR INCONVENIENT?

I hate spiders; you can't trust them. They have too many legs to know where they're going and too many eyes to know where they're looking. I take care of bats, squirrels, opossums, snakes, crocodiles, burglars, and poltergeists. It's my wife's job to handle the spiders.

While you may not share my fear of spiders, seeing one of these little monsters in your kitchen might still cause a feeling of overall disgust and make you want to kill it.

Before you squash that next spider, remember that, in some ways, spiders are actually quite good for the world, which prompts the question "Are they evil or merely inconvenient?"

Did you know that a single spider eats around 2,000 insects every year? If we squashed every spider into extinction, humanity would face extinction, because the insects spiders ordinarily eat would devour our food supply.* No spiders means no people.

Spiders aren't evil; they're inconvenient. The world needs them to control the insect population. We just don't want them crawling around in our ears while we sleep at night.

Evil is something different. Examples of evil are murder, rape, racism, fascism, fat-free ice cream, and many other hideous monstrosities. Those things serve no purpose, other than causing harm. Nonetheless, we can learn something from every experience.

- I failed in business; it was terrible.
- I was born with learning disabilities; I didn't deserve it.
- I've been abused; it was also undeserved.
- I've had my heart broken; it was painful.
- I've lost loved ones; it didn't make sense.
- I've been angry at God.
- I've hated others.
- I've hated myself.

---

* Brian Palmer, "The Case for Spider Conservation: They Keep Pests From Devouring Humans' Food Supply," *the Washington Post*, published on July 21, 2014, https://www.washingtonpost.com/national/health-science/ the-case-for-spider-conservation-they-keep-pests-from-devouring-humans-food- supply/2014/07/21/07b0a21e-0b8c-11e4-8341-b8072b1e7348_story.html.

I've learned that I can use even the worst parts of those experiences to grow if I choose to.

When I was five years old, I was sexually molested; it was evil. I wouldn't wish it on my worst enemy. The pain and trauma caused by those moments echoed in my mind and heart throughout my entire adolescence.

I had a choice. I could allow those moments of extreme trauma to foster pain, bitterness, and hatred in my heart (and it did for a long time). Or I could choose to allow something more beautiful to arise from it. I chose beauty.

With the help of therapy, and the support of my street-view Mentors (who you will learn about later), that experience has given me a deep empathy for others who have also suffered from trauma. I have used it to be a better coach, a better father, and a better citizen.

Was it still evil?

Yes.

Is it our choice to use evil for good?

Yes.

Is it easy?

No.

Is it worth it?

Absolutely.

There is a difference between evil and inconvenient. Regardless of which we're dealing with, we can still learn from our interactions with them.

THE ANTI-MENTOR CHEAT SHEET

Learning from the negative influences in your life comes down to gratitude. Make a concerted effort to choose gratitude over bitterness. A great way to do that is with the Anti-Mentor Cheat Sheet. Take five minutes every day to write down the answers to three questions.

1. **What am I proud of today?** Consider all the things that went well throughout the day, including actions committed by others. You could be proud of something you said or didn't say. Perhaps you're proud of the way a friend handled conflict, or something you or a loved one accomplished. They don't have to be Nobel Prize-worthy accomplishments. Think carefully and write down *everything* that you were proud of today.

2. **What brought me unrest today?** Write down all the things that frustrated you. Maybe somebody angered

you with their words or dismissed your ability to manage a situation. Perhaps you wore a red sweater to shop at Target, and another customer mistakenly asked you where they could find the Cheez-Whiz. Also, don't limit yourself to people with this exercise. Sometimes frustration and anger can come from circumstances. People and circumstances can be equally upsetting. Write them all down.

3. **What are the good and bad things that happened here to teach me?** This is the most important question on the Anti-Mentor Cheat Sheet. Writing down what you learned from your daily experiences gives you the awareness to take action that will lead to momentum.

The purpose of the cheat sheet is to see—on paper, on purpose—all the ways to turn negativity into gratitude and growth and to drive awareness for how the inconveniences of life can help you become better every day.

Getting away from an irritating coworker is only a short-term fix, like putting a Band-Aid on a bullet wound. It might stop the bleeding for a brief moment, but eventually, you'll need to face the issue. Soon, that same type of person will sashay back into your life. They might look different and have a different name. Trust me, they will show up again... and again...and again.

What if these types of people are sent by God as a way for

us to grow and identify areas of growth? Think of it like a doctor who presses down on your broken arm and asks, "Does it hurt when I do this?" The answer is "Ouch, yes!"

Certain types of people will always seem—to us—like they're pressing on our pain points. If we allow them, they could be showing us a wound that we need to heal. Instead of seeing them as demons, let them help you identify areas for growth by taking your medicine.

I'm not saying you shouldn't set boundaries and keep your distance from select individuals. What I am saying is don't just run away from anti-mentors. Figure out what caused you to have that internal reaction and fix it. This is similar to repeating the ninth grade in school if you don't learn the lessons sufficiently to pass the tests. Stop focusing on how much you hate being tested and start focusing on learning the lessons.

Living with gratitude and understanding makes it easier to accept the role of anti-mentors in our lives, learn from them, forgive them, and grow from our experiences with them. Zen Buddhist spiritual icon Thich Nhat Hanh once said, "No mud, no lotus." In layman's terms, you can't find the happiness of the lotus without suffering through the mud. Get in the mud with your anti-mentors, and you will blossom.

PREMEDITATE FORGIVENESS

One of the powerful lessons I've learned is that forgiveness doesn't need to wait until I've been wronged. Tremendous personal development is achieved by forgiving yourself and others for bad deeds or poor choices. Legendary comic Lily Tomlin framed this idea wonderfully when she said, "Forgiveness means giving up all hope for a better past." Read that quote again, and really think about what you might be holding onto that you can't change. Maybe it's time to give up hope that the past will change, and start focusing on a better future.

Lily's quote speaks to acceptance. Once we accept what's happened, we become free to move forward. That's the first step. After acceptance, we must to learn to love the positive and negative events of our past. That will spur compassion and empathy. Increasing our aptitude for those emotions is clear signs of personal growth.

What good does it do to spend today wishing the past to be different? The past never changes. Of much greater impact is to develop the courage to accept the past as-is, learn from it, and move forward.

Chances are you know someone will rile you up next week. Think about it. You likely have a situation at work, at home, in traffic, at church, or somewhere else that will make you angry over the next few days. If that's the case, why wait for it to happen? Instead of reacting in the moment without any thought, try to premeditate forgiveness. If you wait for someone to push your buttons, it will be difficult not to react negatively. If you prepare for it, you'll be ready to act with compassion and empathy.

In 2011, I learned a lot about forgiveness from business-related family drama.

I was born as the third generation in my grandfather's business. My entire childhood was spent going to, coming from, or talking about the furniture store. We were all furniture all the time. My grandfather (the founder) had five locations, and my parents ran one of them.

After being in the business (as an adult) for five years, I realized it wasn't for me. Not because I wasn't good at it. The furniture business wasn't for me because I *hated* it. It wasn't fun. Despite the fact that my grandfather taught me all about the business, I just wasn't passionate about furniture (anymore). So I decided it was time for a change.

Sometimes, a multigenerational family business can become synonymous with the family. You can't talk about the business without talking about family, and you can't talk about the family without talking about the business. After a while, the two entities get so close, you can't tell them apart.

So when I decided to leave the business, many of my family members seemed to feel like I was also leaving the family. As you can imagine, there were lots of hurtful words and hurt feelings. It took years to recover, and we are still in recovery.

In 2011, I experienced the toughest year of my life. It was also a year that provided one of the most valuable learning experiences I've ever had. I underwent tremendous regeneration and redirection in that time frame. I also gained unprecedented momentum and growth.

With 100 percent honesty, I can look back on that period with immense gratitude. I can also say that the experience helped me become a better husband, father, friend, and businessperson. Perhaps most importantly, that tough time taught me a lot about my own resilience, independence, empathy, and ultimately forgiveness.

It's easy to look at an altercation like that with outrage and anger. Once we look at things from the perspective of the other side, empathy and compassion can work their way into our development.

After thinking deeply about why my family acted the way it did about my leaving the business, I saw things a little differently. I finally accepted the past and grew from it. I was able to accept the behind-the-scenes issues that likely affected their reaction to my decision.

If I had not experienced the repercussions of leaving my family's business in 2011, I would not be the person I am today.

Another way to think about forgiveness is to know that when people hurt us, they do it to themselves; we just happen to be in their way. Recently I heard someone say that we are not punished *for* our anger; we are punished *by* it.

When someone wrongs you, they're usually protecting something about themselves. They have a vulnerability, trauma, or fear about a circumstance in which you're involved. In that case, you're collateral damage, not the target of their attack. Unfortunately, just because the bullet wasn't meant for you doesn't mean it didn't strike with the same pain. This reminds me of a story I heard as a kid.

> Two twin brothers once lived in the same home with the same parents and had many of the same experiences growing up. Unfortunately, their father was an alcoholic and had a habit of abusing the boys and their mother. This made much of the boys' life a living hell.
>
> When they were in high school, their father died. It's sad to say, but it caused a sense of relief that washed over the family. Wanting to get as far away from the memories of their father as possible, the boys escaped to college as soon as they graduated from high school. In their haste, they lost touch with

each other. Over time, they drifted further apart, until it had been decades since they last spoke.

In that time, one of the brothers had become an incredibly wealthy businessperson with a net worth in the millions. Because of his rise to wealth and fame, a journalist visited him for an interview to be published in a national journal.

During the interview, the journalist asked him, "What gave you the drive to acquire so much success?"

The twin brother turned massively wealthy businessperson simply replied, "Because my father was an alcoholic; that is why I have become who I am today."

With the rags to riches story in hand, the journalist wondered what had become of the other brother, so she set out to find him. After weeks of searching, she finally found him living in the same city. He wasn't like the wealthy businessperson she interviewed, though; he lived in a broken-down house that smelled of body odor, urine, and drug residue.

As the journalist looked at him she could see the resemblance to the other brother, except for the bruises, track marks from heroin needles, and years of hard living that leathered his skin.

She asked him, "Sir, I met your brother a few weeks ago and

he has become a wealthy and important businessperson. How in the world did you end up like this?"

The man simply replied in his raspy and broken voice, "Because my father was an alcoholic; that is why I have become who I am today.

As it was told to me, the moral of the story was meant to be how one can make something of themselves from difficult and painful beginnings. The rich man was supposed to be celebrated for his focus and ability to pull himself up by his bootstraps and become a self-made man. As I have spent the past few decades thinking about this story, I think there is a deeper meaning.

Both brothers lost; one chased wealth and fame, while the other chased drugs and pleasure. Both used pain and anger to fuel them. When pain, anger, and bitterness provide our fuel, we might get to where we want to go, but at what price? We might acquire some wonderful things and receive a lot of attention, but if we're eaten up with pain on the inside, does it even matter?

At least the poor brother from the story knew he was losing. The rich brother was in hell and didn't even know it. When we live our lives to prove ourselves or to be better than others, we forfeit the greatest blessings and joys in life.

Let's enjoy the journey by forgiving those who have hurt and traumatized us so that we can enjoy the life we've been given.

CURIOSITY OVER JUDGEMENT

Choosing to be curious over judgmental is key to reacting more positively to the anti-mentors in our lives. When we're curious, we're never judgmental; when we're judgmental, we're never curious. A judgment is a decision; it's final and external. Nothing is more capable of stunting personal growth than being judgmental.

When we make a final decision about anything in a state of evolution, even if we're right, we become wrong eventually. Instead of saying, "This person is foolish," try saying, "This person is acting foolishly *for now*. Let's see what happens."

We can't accurately judge a person or circumstance, because judgments are stagnant. By contrast, people and circumstances are always changing. This contradiction is best represented by a quote from the father of American psychology, Horace Mann: "Do not think of knocking out another person's brains because he differs in opinion from you. It would be as rational to knock yourself on the head because you differ from yourself ten years ago."

I would be unrecognizable to someone who spent time with

me ten years ago. You might be the same way. People and circumstances change. It's nonsensical to judge anyone, because in ten years, they're probably going to be much different. Instead, approach people and circumstances with curiosity. That way, you'll be able to ask questions that open a new realm of possibilities.

> ## TURN INSIGHT INTO ACTION
>
> We can't judge people for their actions and expect them to judge us for our intentions. So who do you need to forgive? Maybe it's a family member, an old friend, or an ex-love; maybe it's *you*. Forgive someone today.

Curiosity over judgment also means responding with compassion. When someone is rude or insults you, ask yourself what that person might be going through. Think back to a time when you acted like that. Why did you do it? Were you going through something? Well, other people go through tough times, too. They might have money troubles. Maybe they just got out of a bad relationship. Perhaps their boss is making their job unbearable. Worst of all, they might have inserted money into a vending machine and pushed the button for the Snickers bar they desperately needed, and it got stuck.

THERMOMETERS VERSUS THERMOSTATS

Sick people need medicine to get better, and bad behavior

is a symptom of someone's emotional, physical, or spiritual sickness. By reflecting someone's negative energy back at them, we'll make them sicker. Instead, give them a healthy dose of compassion, kindness, and empathy to help them get well. Even if they don't get better, at least we won't make them any sicker.

Consider the purpose of a thermometer versus that of a thermostat. The purpose of a thermometer is strictly to provide a temperature reading. Many people approach interactions with others as if they are only using a thermometer. If they detect a hot situation with the potential for anger and hostility, they rise to meet those specifications in their communication with the other individual. If the reading is cold with disengagement and disinterest, their communication will fall to meet that level of the interaction.

The purpose of a thermostat is a little more complex. If the thermostat detects a hot environment, it will start working to create a more comfortable temperature. Are we a victim of our circumstance, where we match the emotional heat to our environment? Or are we willing, through awareness and understanding, to recognize the circumstance and then work to create a better interaction.

A favorite mantra of mine that helps me stay aligned with this concept is "I will be who I am no matter who stands before me." It means that I decide who I am up front, and it doesn't matter with whom I'm interacting, because I am who I am and I will not rise to the level of a heated conversation or fall to a lower expectation for the interaction.

We have the power to choose to act with kindness, empathy, and compassion, no matter who stands before us.

THE ANTI-MENTOR IN ALL OF US

Sometimes, it helps to put ourselves in the perspective of the anti-mentor. On the occasions I've acted out of anger or frustration, while under a lot of stress or uncertainty in my life, I was too preoccupied to be thoughtful or compassionate.

Strangely, we judge people based on their *actions*, yet expect them to judge us based on our *intentions*. If we were curious enough to wonder about others' intentions, we would almost always realize that they're not out to hurt us at all. They're doing the best they can with what they have at the time.

Think about curiosity as the antidote for judgment. Less judgment and more curiosity in the world could lead to amazing things. Choose curiosity over judgment today and see it how it feels.

CHAPTER 5

THE MICRO-MENTOR

"In my walks, every man I meet is my superior in some way, and in that I learn from him."

—RALPH WALDO EMERSON

A misconception about mentorship is that we only find it within the ivory towers of Fortune 500 companies or the hallowed halls of Ivy League universities. That's simply not true. Opportunities for mentorship already exist all around us.

Every person, circumstance, and interaction has the potential to teach us something. That is the essence of the micro-mentor. The opportunities to learn, grow, and develop come and go throughout our day, no matter who we are, where we go, or when we get there. No contract is needed, and we don't need permission.

Sometimes, mentorship moments happen at the family dinner table, during your morning commute, or simply while walking down the street. You never know when an impactful situation will arise. The key is to be aware and open to the possibilities.

Sit outside a coffee shop for an hour. You might notice the way another patron stands tall in line and orders with confidence. Would that demeanor look good on you?

Perhaps the way the barista smiles when they hand you a six-dollar coffee is impressive.

You might pay special attention to the way someone eliminates all the distractions around them and focuses intently on their laptop for work. That truly is an art form, because productivity killers are all over the place at any coffee shop. Consider that hideous jazz fusion/adult contemporary/nothingness music they pipe into the sound system. There's also the person who orders a triple foam, nonfat, left-handed, high-octane, hyper-supernova-latte with a caramel drizzle and three pumps of magic dust. How can anyone not be a little disturbed by the reality of those things? Some people have a gift. Maybe you can figure out how they do it, just by watching them.

If coffee isn't your thing, try browsing the aisles at Target in the middle of the afternoon. Look carefully, and you'll notice the way different people make purchase decisions. Did any employee have an effect on *your* willingness to buy something when you walked in the door? Everyday life is an excellent training ground if you're paying attention.

ENTHUSIASTIC DISCOVERY

We can learn, grow, and develop from *every* person; they don't even need to be adults. I've had some outstanding mentors throughout my lifetime; the two best are my children. By being themselves, they've taught me more about life than anybody else.

For example, I have never seen my two-year-old, Kendrick, worry about his retirement savings. I have also never seen him dwell on something in his past. His mind, body, and spirit are always aligned in the present.

When adults see difference, we fear it. Kendrick sees difference and celebrates it. That is a lesson from which we can all learn.

Likewise, my daughter has an appreciation for how everything works in life. Kendall approaches all her interactions with infinite wonder and curiosity. Every step she takes is filled with ideas of how grass grows, what makes the sky is blue, and why broccoli tastes so dang awful. What would happen if we had the same approach?

My daughter has taught me how to appreciate all the things in life that most adults take for granted. That level of curiosity comes naturally to kids. Unfortunately, the path to adulthood often beats it out of us, as we get so concerned with the daily stresses of life we lose our enthusiastic discovery.

Kendall is a walking example for enthusiastic discovery. There is nothing in her life that she doesn't wonder about and explore.

TURN INSIGHT INTO ACTION

Watch the look on a toddler's face when they discover something new. That look of excitement (from their incredible achievement) and curiosity (about the places they can go and things they can do now) is enthusiastic discovery at its best.

In what ways could you apply that type of curiosity this week?

INTERROBANG ?

In 1962, the head of an advertising agency, Martin K. Speckter, proposed using a single punctuation mark called the interrobang (?). He simply combined a question mark with an exclamation point. Nonetheless, it addressed a need, which was to convey excitement and inquiry with one symbol. He thought copywriters could use it in advertising materials to most accurately and efficiently express this unique emotion to the target audience.

Today, I'm not sure how many people use the interrobang with regularity. I just think it's a cool way to express the idea of enthusiastic discovery. It's a good reminder to be enthusiastic about discovering new ways to see the world.

Imagine getting an offer letter for your dream job. It's everything you ever wanted from a career perspective! The pay is great; you get to do work in what you're passionate about; and you love the people you'll be working with.

First of all, you're thrilled to have the opportunity. At the same time, you might have a lot of questions about what that means: What will my office be like? Who will I meet while I'm there? How challenging will the work be? How will my bonus be structured?

The questions are limitless; so are the possibilities.

By living with enthusiastic discovery, you'll see a massive change in the way you see yourself, other people, and other things. The next time you go for a walk outside, you might think about who else has walked in that area. You might wonder about the rock beneath the surface with water flowing beneath that ground, and fire underneath all of it. Thinking deeply like that creates a connection to everything around you.

Enthusiastic discovery can also be used to handle particularly tricky personal encounters, like those we discussed in the previous chapter.

When we interact with someone who becomes confrontational or insulting, we *try* to remember not to take it personally. Stop for a moment and wonder why a person would think they can get what they want by treating people so poorly. By doing that, we might uncover some problems occurring *behind the scenes* in their lives. Consequently, we might react with compassion rather than outrage; this alone could be enough to transform the conversation from adversarial to something much more meaningful.

People who treat others with hostility are likely to be dealing with serious problems in their lives. Even if they seem like they have everything going for them, chances are that there is something in the background that is causing them a tremendous amount of pain. They could have a lot of stress at work. Perhaps their marriage is failing. Maybe their kids are in serious trouble. They could be sick, or someone they love could be dying. Many people have mental health issues, ongoing struggles with addiction, physical pain, and other brutal issues they may be dealing with. Living with these things is punishment enough.

> ## TURN INSIGHT INTO ACTION
>
> There is no such thing as good and bad people; there are only joyous people and miserable people. When people are joyful, they take actions we categorize as good; when people are miserable, they take actions we categorize as bad.
>
> Good and bad has nothing to do with who we are; they're all about what we do. When we see people acting badly, that should be a sign that something is making them miserable. We wouldn't try to save a drowning person by pushing them further underwater, so we should try reacting to the hostility of others with compassion and see if their better self doesn't rise to the surface accordingly.

There could be a thousand reasons why a person would act with hostility. It also might be something in that person's past that has always haunted them. Some people daily deal with their traumatic childhood memories. By responding with enthusiastic discovery instead of anger, we open ourselves up to more insight, followed by understanding, empathy, and a much better interaction.

It can be difficult to maintain enthusiastic discovery in the face of confrontational behavior, especially in today's always-on-the-go, two-lane fast-food drive-thru world. The competition is fierce to be first in a society that overvalues overworking. Aggression is only one side effect of the speed at which today's society moves. Another is something referred to as hustle culture.

THE ABSURDITY OF HUSTLE CULTURE

Enthusiastic Discovery

Many of us are <u>too busy hustling to practice enthusiastic discovery.</u> Let's take some time to think about hustle culture and ask some important questions: Is that really how we want to live? Is it getting us to where we want to be? What will we do when we arrive? Are we happy? Satisfied? Fulfilled? What about downtime and our mental health?

> ### TURN INSIGHT INTO ACTION
>
> When was the last time you indulged in a great book, beautiful music, or a fun movie; shared a laugh with someone you love; or just sat?
>
> French philosopher <u>Blaise Pascal</u> once said, <u>"All of humanity's problems stem from man's inability to sit quietly in a room alone."</u>

When I was in the furniture business, if an item became exceedingly popular, I could order more inventory; problem solved. Our time is quite different. We all get twenty-four hours in a day as personal inventory. We can't simply order more of it.

A distinction exists between meaningful time and busywork. We must be deliberately active about using our inventory of personal time well. Some time needs to be allocated toward business and some for leisure. We must understand that our inventory is limited and distribute it accordingly.

Some resoundingly successful businesspeople have fallen

victim to hustle culture, thinking success is defined by working twenty hours per day, sleeping sparingly, and eating on the run.

Hustle culture is an epidemic stemming from the competition in all industries that has dramatically intensified. This is a big downside of democratic, capitalistic society. As Winston Churchill once so eloquently said, "Democracy is the worst form of government, except for all those other forms that have been tried from time to time."

As a result, people are medicating themselves solely to speed up and wind down instantly, as if a few extra minutes at the start and end of each day are a crime.

Energy drinks have become the mid-afternoon snack of corporate warriors all over the world. Instead of powering up with a sensible balance of carbs and protein, people in thousand-dollar business suits walk around with a briefcase in one hand and an energy drink in the other.

TURN INSIGHT INTO ACTION

Hustling isn't innately bad. I take a lot of pride in working really hard. Anything taken to an extreme that reduces our joy for life is the problem.

In what ways could overdoing it be negatively affecting your mind, body, and spirit?

The real victims of hustle culture describe their daily routine as "grinding." They say, "Hey, I'm grinding it out." When something grinds, it's breaking. The resulting sound of gears grinding in your car means your transmission is about to blow up. With that in mind, what is happening when the human body and mind are grinding?

The biggest impetus for hustle culture is to acquire material success. People get too focused on their social stature, when the discoveries they should be most enthusiastic about are free. Jesus said, "For what does it profit a man to gain the whole world, and forfeit his soul?"

Our legacy and the people we impact have value that lives beyond us. For instance, the few minutes I spend with my kids right before they go to sleep at night are often the most valuable moments of my day. They can also be the toughest, because by that point, I've already given so much to my work and other obligations throughout the day. At times, I'm tempted to rush through the process and get to the part of the evening when I can relax. I often have to remind myself that a deep and meaningful relationship with a significant other, child, or close friend is infinitely more rewarding than any material possession.

Whatever your ideal success looks like, take the time to enjoy the roads it takes to get there. If the people closest to you are your most cherished things in life, enjoy every interaction with them. If a good friend is important enough to take thirty minutes out of your busy day to enjoy a coffee together, be present in those thirty minutes. Don't think about all the work you have to do when your coffee time is over. Enjoy the break with your friend. Listen, learn, and engage. Be in the moment.

There's an old Chinese proverb that says, "The journey is better than the destination." If that's true, and our ultimate destination is death, why waste this journey by *not* enjoying everything we possibly can?

You might consider working to be your passion. If that's the case, enjoy it. Lori Greiner of *Shark Tank* once said, "Entrepreneurs are the only people who will work eighty hours a week to avoid working forty hours a week." This is different than working solely to acquire material possessions. In this case, you're passionate about the work you're doing; you enjoy it. The important thing is to know what makes you happy. It also doesn't matter if you're happy working those eighty hours a week or working just enough to make ends meet. Know yourself well enough to practice enthusiastic discovery during your journey.

When we reach a long-term goal or destination, a strange phenomenon is that the worst time of our lives can occur immediately after. Many athletes have sunk into a deep depression after winning championships because they're left with a feeling of emptiness. They've lived their entire lives with a singular goal—to achieve the highest level of success within their sport. When that mission is over, they're left searching to fill a void.

This idea is not limited to world-class athletes. We work towards goals all the time. Maybe we desire a luxury car; a home in the suburbs; or a once-in-a-lifetime, luxurious vacation. The problem is that once we achieve any of those things, an emptiness replaces them. That takes us into a never-ending cycle of chasing one item of short-term gratification after another. To make matters worse, the more you have, the more you stand to lose. At that point, fear takes over—a fear of losing our stockpile of stuff.

We should always strive for achievement. Let's just be careful to not obsess over items that provide mostly an immediate value as the only things that matter in life.

AFFIRM TRUTH, NO MATTER WHERE YOU FIND IT

Another important aspect of enthusiastic discovery is always keeping our mind open to other ideas, perspectives, and experiences. This means we affirm truth, no matter where we find it.

Too often, we close our minds to people or things that are unfamiliar to us. We all have pre-existing notions of truth. Different cultures, religions, and political affiliations all have their doctrine that tells people what is right and wrong. Living with enthusiastic discovery means we're willing to suspend those beliefs to listen to others without judgement. We must be willing to consider things that contradict our foundation of truth to experience real personal growth.

Rather than shut those out who live, worship, and believe differently, approach them with curiosity. See what you can learn from them. If they're open to it, you might be able to help them learn something as well. Imagine the possibilities if the 7 billion people in the world all had this approach.

THINKING IS GREAT; ACTION IS BETTER

Spiritual writer and Franciscan friar Richard Rohr once said, "We do not think ourselves into new ways of living, we live ourselves into new ways of thinking."

Soliciting the experiences of others, leveraging your own, and finding mentorship at the microlevel is only as good as the actions you take. Once you discover new ways to think, you must *live* them.

Ideas are like trying new clothes. You try them on and see how they look and feel on you. If they fit, you keep them; if they don't, you simply put them back on the rack. Remember, life isn't a one-size-fits-all situation. If something doesn't fit *you*, that doesn't mean it won't fit *someone else*.

If we only acquire knowledge and never take action, we risk living our final days with regret. Embrace the idea of the micro-mentor. Then, take action. Without action, none of it means anything.

In John 8:32, Jesus said, "And you will know the truth, and the truth will make you free." The context of this passage speaks to experiential knowledge, meaning your experience will prove the truth of your actions. Only then will you come to believe that truth.

Let's fast-forward a couple of thousand years by going from the immortal lessons of Jesus Christ to the much less personal, yet easily accessible, words of Siri. In the next chapter, you'll learn how to leverage modern-day technology as the most powerful knowledge enhancement advantage of all time.

CHAPTER 6

THE DIGITAL MENTOR

"The Internet doesn't care that you're not interested in learning. It will continue to evolve without you."

—GARY VAYNERCHUK

If you could have a fifteen-minute mentorship conversation with anyone living or dead, who would you choose?

Imagine being able to learn from Steve Jobs, Michael Jordan, Martin Luther King Jr., Jesus Christ, Buddha, or Muhammad.

Maybe you just want to pick the brain of the guy who invented the Chia Pet. Fun fact: his name is Joseph Pedott, and he is also the founder of the company who successfully marketed The Clapper.

Suppose you could hop into a time machine that could make that happen. What an amazing opportunity, right‽ (That interrobang sure is a handy symbol.)

The good news is that this opportunity already exists. All you need to do is open a browser on your laptop, tablet, or smartphone, and you can absorb the most powerful lessons from the most thought-provoking leaders.

If you have internet access, you have everything you need to get started. It's that simple. The world is at your fingertips in a way that it has never been before in the history of humankind.

Want to know how to bake the perfect souffle? YouTube can show you everything from folding the egg whites to when to take its puffy deliciousness out of the oven.

How about something a little more complicated, like performing brain surgery? I don't recommend attempting it unless you're already a trained, certified, and highly skilled neurosurgeon. In which case, if you need a quick refresher, the videos are available. I'm not kidding. Before you spend $450,000 to become a brain surgeon, a good first step would be to go to YouTube, watch what it looks like, and see if you can even stomach it. If you pass out, spending money on medical school isn't going to help.

The internet can show you how to do just about anything.

Some have used it to accomplish amazing things. One of my favorite examples of leveraging technology as a mentor comes from a man named Julius Yego.

MR. YOUTUBE

You might have heard of Julius Yego before. He is called Mr. YouTube. If you don't know his story, you *should*. His story is motivating, inspiring, and amazing.

In 1989, Julius Yego was born in a remote farming village in Kenya. He and his family lived there with no electricity. It was basic shelter that provided a roof over their heads—a place to sleep, eat, and nothing more.

Julius was stocky and not an exceptional runner. His frame was remarkably different from other Kenyan athletes, who traditionally dominated the world of distance running with their lean, athletic builds. That wasn't about to stop him from pursuing his passion.

Julius was also determined to not let the absence of technology in his home limit his potential. He made regular trips to something called a *cyber* in the nearest city. In case you're not familiar with a cyber, it's like a library without books. People in Kenya and some other countries use cybers for internet access. This is where and how Julius discovered the power of YouTube.

Something about throwing a javelin interested Julius, perhaps because it was a sport in which he could compete without having the traditional lean, athletic body type of his fellow countrymen.

At the cyber, Julius watched countless videos of the world's greatest javelin throwers. He studied their techniques and tried to apply everything he learned when he got home.

At home, Julius practiced with wooden sticks for javelins. "When you don't have the facilities, you improvise with what you have," Julius said. Being determined to make it work, he worked with whatever he could scrounge up around his village.

Not too long after, Julius competed and became the first athlete in Kenya's history to win the African Games' javelin event. At that point, he was finally given some resources like a highly skilled coach, professional javelins for practice, a proper training facility, and opportunities to compete that he never had before.

In 2016, Julius Yego won the silver medal for Kenya in the Rio de Janeiro Olympic Games. He became the second-best javelin thrower in the universe! Julius made it happen because he had the will to succeed and didn't let a lack of resources stop him. The odds were astronomically high against him being able to compete at even the lowest levels of javelin competition. Rather than admitting defeat with a victim's mindset, he approached his passion with enthusiastic discovery and effectively leveraged technology to fulfill his dream.

TECHNOLOGY IS AMORAL

We view technology through one of two lenses. One lens presents technology as the be-all and end-all, as if all of life's answers are always found in the warm, inviting glow of an electronic screen. This lens reflects the words of immortal philosopher Homer Simpson, who once said, "The answers to life's problems aren't at the bottom of a bottle. They're on TV."

The other lens with which we could view technology is to see it as a powerful tool capable of causing mass chaos, one that could spur the end of civilization. For this viewpoint, consider what Stephen Hawking had to say about the evolution of artificial intelligence: "Success in creating AI would be the biggest event in human history. Unfortunately, it might also be the last, unless we learn how to avoid the risks."

I'm not saying we should abolish the words of one of the greatest minds in recent history...or those of Stephen Hawking. (See what I did there?) What I am saying is that technology is amoral, meaning it is neither good nor bad. The impact of technology is dependent on how it's used.

The internet is nothing more than a tool for us to either build you up or break you down. It can be used for good when learning about kindness and altruism from Mother Teresa. On the other hand, the internet can be used for bad when surfing the dark web to build a massive mechanical sphere that blocks out the sun (ala Montgomery Burns, also from *The Simpsons*. Is there nothing an episode of *The Simpsons* can't teach us?).

A variety of things exist in the world that could help or hurt depending on how they're used.

You need food to fuel your body. If Big Macs are your primary source of nutrition, that will cause the food to become a negative influence in your body. By all means, have a Big Mac once in a while if you enjoy them. I'm not here to recommend abolishing all the guilty pleasures in life. Balance that indulgence with a salad or green vegetable more often throughout the week.

Food, politics, medication, and sex can all be used for good and healthy purposes. Or they can be used as tools that erode the very fabric of society. Will these things be a blessing or a curse in your life? The choice is yours.

William James once said, "Our greatest power is the power to choose." Technology is no different. The way you interact with it will determine whether you're building something better for yourself and others or breaking something down. Which result do you want to be a part of?

At the time of this writing, we are in the COVID-19 pandemic. Thankfully, the internet has enabled millions of people to work from home. The impact of that alone is massive. In this extremely challenging time, the internet has saved millions of families, if not the world. Without it, productivity losses would be exponentially higher. There would be no work from home, no online deliveries of essential products, and perhaps worst of all, no video entertainment for the kids.

During previous epidemics, there were few activities to keep kids educated. In 2020, technology has allowed us the ability to connect in ways we wouldn't have been able to only a few short decades ago.

COMPARISON IS COUNTERPRODUCTIVE

One of the most polarizing subgenres of technology is social media. You either see it as nothing more than an obnoxious sounding board to voice religious and political agendas or you spend countless nighttime hours browsing the pages of family members, friends, and neighbors until you wake up to a tablet or phone falling on your face.

Think deeply when your connections post nonstop pictures of their family's success stories. Most people are eager to post pictures of their children winning academic honors and earning athletic achievements. They're happy to parade videos of their baby doing something unbelievably adorable or shockingly intelligent. "Holy buckets! Look at how advanced he is for his age!" is what they want you to see, think, and feel. At the same you get the lovely side effect of an inferiority complex regarding your #ParentingSkills.

What you don't see on their social media accounts is the reality of their daily lives. If behind the scenes footage of that highlight reel existed, you might see their teenage daughter get busted for breaking curfew (#ParentFail), their younger son getting detention for being disruptive in class (#SummerSchool), and their adorable baby whipping bowls of SpaghettiOs all over the kitchen (#BossBaby).

Former president Theodore Roosevelt once said, "Comparison is the thief of joy." Those immortal words ring remarkably true when thinking about the impact of social media on your state of mind.

Life is not all sunshine and rainbows. The key is to not allow other people's social media accounts convince you that it should be. *Don't compare your reality to someone else's highlight reel.*

TEN SECONDS OF PEACE

For all the good things that technology can do for us, it's important to exercise moderation. Too much of anything is bad. Eat too much cake, and you'll get sick. Watch too much television, and you'll become inactive and lethargic. Even too much water is a problem; actually, you can die from drinking too much water.

> **TURN INSIGHT INTO ACTION**
>
> When you go to bed this evening, take a few moments to reflect on the day. What discoveries did you make? What went well? What did *not* go well? What impact did you have, and what impact did the day have on you?

When your eyes first open in the morning, don't jump out of bed. Pause for the first ten seconds to create a moment of intention. Think about what you want your day to look like. How do you want to show up for other people? What kind of discoveries could you make? What impact do you want to have?

Those ten seconds of reflection and intention aren't anything new. For thousands of years, people have been saying their prayers at night as a way of aligning themselves with their creator. Someone once said that prayer isn't something you do; it's something you become. I believe wholeheartedly in that statement.

None of this means you should quit your job the next morning if you reflect on your job at night and discover you're not happy. It means you begin by making small, gradual, and consistent changes.

If you aren't where you want to be, ask yourself what actions you need to take that will give you the momentum to start heading in a different direction that will achieve different results.

TURN INSIGHT INTO ACTION

You may notice that I never use the phrase, "Live your best life." There is no such thing as a "best life." You can only get better every day, which is great news!

If there was a best life, what would you do once you got there? There would be no reason to carry on because your life would already be the best it possibly could be, as if you defeated life. You won! Game over.

Take a few moments to consider how you can make your life better. What characteristics, actions, and attitudes (when applied consistently) will give you the best possible outcomes?

Instead of trying to live the impossible *best* life, focus on living your best day today. That doesn't mean that everything goes perfectly; it means you take full advantage of every moment with gratitude and love the day. Today is all we have. The past doesn't exist any longer, and the future is never a promise. One day, we will all die, and it will happen sooner than we expect.

Let's learn, grow, and develop from the limitless possibilities provided by technology. Use your powers for good, not evil. This same approach should be considered when reading the next chapter about the categorical mentor.

CHAPTER 7

THE CATEGORICAL MENTOR

> *"I saw the angel in the marble and carved until I set him free."*
> —MICHELANGELO

Legend has it that an admirer of Michelangelo's work once asked him how he was able to produce the statue of David from nothing more than a twenty-foot slab of Carrara marble. The artist responded with the famous quote that kicks off this chapter.

Picture yourself as Michelangelo for a moment. Visualize a large cement block in the middle of the room. Your job is to shape a masterpiece from that two-ton slab of rock by chiseling out the undesirable pieces. This is the essence of the categorical mentor.

When working with mentors, we must remember everyone

has flaws. Everyone. Some of the world's most brilliant and influential people have had struggles with money, addiction, and infidelity; some were just plain jerks. Just because they have what we want doesn't mean we should do what they've done.

TURN INSIGHT INTO ACTION

Success must be determined by more than what people think of us, what we acquire, or what our social status is. It is also dependent on physical health, emotional well-being, family stability, and how well you treat people. There may be other ways you define success as well. Everybody has different qualifications.

Your personal brand is found at the intersection between who you really are and who others perceive you to be. Once again, a choice exists where you can focus on the perception of others and pull reality into it or you can focus on who you really are and allow perception to take care of itself. Which will you choose?

We might be tempted to follow the example of today's most popular celebrities and social media personalities, hoping to emulate their success. Such an effort will most likely obliterate your soul because it's concentrated heavily on those material possessions with little to no attention toward building meaningful relationships or achieving any form of long-term fulfillment.

There are some lessons pertaining to success we could learn from those who have developed their fame and fortune. For instance, I'm sure that an hour spent talking to a highly successful social media influencer about digital marketing would be incredibly valuable. This provides a good example of the categorical mentor. Observe their business savvy. Chisel away the parts that will damage your soul.

If a mentor is a brilliant businessperson and lacking in some other areas, it's fine to learn from their professional skills. Be careful not to duplicate their downfalls. Perhaps the greatest businessperson I've ever known on a personal level was my late grandfather.

FROM YARD SALE INNOVATOR TO FURNITURE STORE ENTREPRENEUR

My grandfather was born on a tobacco farm in 1930—the

apex of the Great Depression in America—in Roxboro, North Carolina. His parents were poor tenant farmers.

> Tenant farming is an agricultural production system where the farmers own nothing and do all the work on a farm in exchange for a place to live.
>
> The landlord has all the control in this situation. They reap the overwhelming majority of the monetary value from the farming and perform none of the labor. All they do is contribute their land.

My grandfather had bigger dreams than the farm could provide. He got married, had two kids, and moved to Raleigh, North Carolina, to pursue a different life.

With a wife and two kids to support, his finance job at a local tire sales company was just enough to keep food on the table but left little extra. So he began brainstorming about ways to make extra money.

The first thing he thought of was to have a yard sale. Isn't that the first thing that occurs to most Americans in that situation? When all else fails, sell everything. There was one huge problem with that: he didn't have anything to sell.

Undeterred by a lack of resources, my grandfather thought of a work-around to have his yard sale. He decided to get yesterday's newspaper every week. Old news is free, so that was one way of circumventing the five cents needed to purchase the daily paper as startup capital. When you're broke, every penny counts, especially in those days.

> If you were born any time after the mid 1990s, you might not be familiar with what a newspaper was. Back in the old days—BI (before internet)—you could buy what was basically Twitter in print form. In case you don't know what Twitter is, think of Instagram with just words.
>
> The daily news arrived at your doorstep every morning in rolled-up paper form. It wasn't as instantaneous as getting notifications on your smartphone; it was somewhat of a comforting experience to sit with a cup of coffee and the newspaper every morning.

One of the most popular sections of the newspaper was the classified advertisements section. The purpose of these ads was to sell things from one local citizen to another. Some of them were to announce yard sales. The ads would include the address and phone number of the person having the sale. That way, anyone who was interested in attending could show up at the right time and place.

My grandfather would call each person having a yard sale and say, "Hi, my name is Lawrence. I see that you're having a yard sale this weekend. If you'd like, I'd be happy to come by after the sale is over on Sunday evening and dispose of anything that didn't sell for you. I won't charge you anything."

A lot of people took him up on his offer, and that's how he got his first set of things to sell for his first yard sale.

There was one small detail my grandfather left out when he spoke to these people. Instead of disposing the items, he took them home to sell at his yard sale the following Friday. The old saying is true that "One person's junk is another person's treasure." Just because someone didn't buy the junk in one yard doesn't mean someone else won't buy it from a different yard. This worked surprisingly well for my grandfather. He successfully moved unsold items from one yard sale to his own for a small profit every weekend for about five years. By that time, he had enough money to not only support his family better but also rent a small storefront a stone's throw from downtown Raleigh.

Within five more years, he had made enough money to buy a piece of land on which he built a 14,000-square-foot warehouse in Southeast Raleigh. He stocked that warehouse with brand-new furniture and became one of the region's biggest independent furniture retailers. In the end, my grandfather owned and operated five stores. He also had some commercial and residential real estate.

I have the utmost respect for my grandfather, and I greatly admire his business acumen. He saw opportunities for success and acted on them to create a meaningful company that changed the trajectory of his life.

Despite the obvious success my grandfather built over

the years, if he could do it all over again, I know he would have done some things differently. He probably would have spent more time with his family and taken much better care of his health.

In Chapter 5, I wrote about hustle culture. My grandfather definitely subscribed to that way of life. He worked six days a week, saying, "If God only took one day off, why should I take more?"

In his mind, working harder was the solution to any problem. If I told him I was tired, he would say, "Well, then, you should have worked harder during the day, and you'll sleep better at night."

When I was young, I worked at his warehouse to assemble furniture for him. The problem was that the building had no heat or air conditioning. In the middle of winter, I would work all day, putting parts together for furniture in a freezing cold warehouse. By the end of the day, my hands got so cold I lost feeling in them. Have you ever tried to manipulate tools or use your hands when they're bordering on actual frostbite? It's almost impossible.

One day, I told him, "I can't put anything together anymore today because my hands are frozen." His response: "That means your fingers aren't working hard enough. Working people don't get cold."

That response used to drive me crazy. Working harder *was* an option; so was giving me the space heater from his office for a few hours. That "work harder" philosophy was something my grandfather may have believed in too strongly.

TURN INSIGHT INTO ACTION

Chances are if you've taken the initiative to read this book, you're no stranger to working hard. Still, the idea of "just working harder" is a lie. There are plenty of people who are working incredibly hard (maybe you're one of them) and still feel stuck or unfulfilled in some way(s). Working hard is valuable, but so is working smart.

In what ways could you start working *hard* and *smart*?

My grandfather had his first heart attack at fifty years old, which resulted in open heart surgery. After that, he developed type II diabetes, which he struggled to control for the rest of his life. In 2007, he developed congestive heart failure.

In 2009, my grandfather died at seventy-eight years old. Not only did he suffer for the last twenty-nine years but, in my view, he should have lived for another twenty years.

Toward the final days of his life, my grandfather could barely talk. The congestive heart failure made it sound like he was drowning with every breath he took. Eventually, I saw a millionaire take his last breath. In that moment, there was no concern over the state of the business. His bank accounts, real estate, and financials were nowhere to be found. But I was there, and so was my grandmother and the rest of my family. At the end, he wanted to see what mattered most—the people he loved. If I could have one more conversation with my grandfather, I'm convinced he would have asked me about my family and my health, not my finances and career.

My grandfather was one of many categorical mentors in my life. As with all categorical mentors, learn how to apply the aspects you admire most about these mentors and chisel away the rest. Absorb their strengths, and adjust the things they would likely do differently if they had the chance. If you're like me, you've got plenty of your own shortcomings to deal with anyway.

CHAPTER 8

THE STREET-VIEW MENTOR

"I carry a small sheet of paper in my wallet that has written on it the names of people whose opinions of me matter. To be on that list, you have to love me for my strengths and struggles."

—BRENÉ BROWN

We all make wrong turns when driving the long and winding road of life. Sometimes we drive too fast, and occasionally we even drift across the center line to face extreme danger.

When that happens, it helps to have someone sitting next to you who can grab the wheel and get you back into your lane before an eighteen-wheeler bears down and turns your car with everything in it into a smoking scrap heap.

For me, that person is my wife, Merideth. Others in the car might help as well. One of my kids might scream from the back seat, "Daddy, look out!" A trusted friend might also slap me in the back of my head to alert me in the nick of time.

Those are the people who—for various reasons—have earned the right to have a strong voice in my life; they are my street-view mentors.

Who's riding shotgun in your car?

Have they earned the right to speak up from the back seat?

Most importantly, are you sure *you're* driving the car?

If you're a passenger on your life journey, that's a big problem. For instance, suppose you have aspirations of being an artist, and your parents steer you in the direction of business school instead. They think they know what is best for you (as all well-intentioned parents do) and influence your decision accordingly.

You can love your mom and dad until the end of time; *don't let them drive the car for you.* The same goes for anyone else. Don't allow a teacher, friend, coworker, or anyone else to control your journey.

Many parents love and protect their children into failure, depression, and discontentment. Your loved ones want to protect you. If you let them, you will become a person lacking the character, resilience, and drive to reach your highest potential. American author and professor John Augustus Shedd said it best: "A ship in harbor is safe, but that is not what ships are built for."

If you think someone else is behind the wheel of your life, it's time to take control. Remember, this book will *not* change your life; neither will anybody else. Only *you* can change your life. Others may provide support, but *you* must be the one who does the work. For that to happen, you need to be in the driver's seat. It reminds me of a saying from Saint Augustine: "Pray as though everything depended on God. Work as though everything depended on you."

The street-view mentor's objective is not to drive the car for you; it's to give directions when you've taken a wrong turn or have made some bad decisions. Street-view mentors keep you aligned with your best route when you start to stray.

Another common scenario is to be driving your own car with the wrong people as passengers. When you have people in your car who don't have your best interest at heart, not only will they not help you, they might even purposely try to steer you in the wrong direction.

You're not alone if you need to reevaluate who should be

driving with you on your life journey. Rest assured that a lot of people have terrible best friends; they also have family members who might have good intentions but may not necessarily know what is best for them. Simply being a close relative doesn't give anyone the right to have a strong voice in your life.

Self-interest, addiction, manipulation, and an array of other negative influences can be a part of anybody's life. People who carry those burdens are likely not worthy of being in your car. They're more apt to play bumper cars with your life than they are to help you when you need them most.

Never consider people your street-view mentors by process of elimination. Don't put your best friend in the passenger seat because his gambling addiction is slightly less destructive than the criminal tendencies of your other friends. If nobody suits the job description of the street-view mentor, keep looking; someone will surface eventually. If not, you're better off traveling alone for a while. It's better to drive alone than to be in a car full of axe murderers and psychopaths.

The ideal situation is to have people in the car who have your best interest at heart. Street-view mentors have listened to you, and you've listened to them. They share similar values, and they're close enough to know when you're veering off track.

FILTERS

Occasionally giving up your power to the people riding in your car is okay. There are times when I look to my wife, Merideth, for guidance on a personal issue, and I know she will help me to make the best possible decision.

Street-view mentors (like Merideth in my situation) know us so well they're capable of providing reliable and trustworthy direction when we need it most. They'll also hold us accountable by letting us know when we're doing something that doesn't make a lot of sense. Sometimes they're right and we need to change. Other times, the challenge helps us to think through our decisions more deeply. Either way, street-view mentors are imperative for our journey. Similarly, they'll be happy to affirm our good choices. When we receive guidance from anyone else, we should always consider the source before acting on it.

Ask yourself if the source of criticism or affirmation has earned the right to speak into your life. Either way, just because you get guidance from someone you don't like or from someone who isn't a street-view mentor doesn't mean it's not true.

After we consider the source, we also need to ask ourselves what we can learn from the interaction. It doesn't matter if our best friend or worst enemy provided the guidance; it only matters if there is truth to the lesson.

The truth, even when it's spoken by your enemy, is still the truth. Instead of granting carte blanche to everyone who has insight for us, we must apply appropriate filters regarding *source* and *truth* to those who haven't earned the right to speak up yet. Some additional commonsense questions can also be applied as filters.

- Does the person have a history of being manipulative?
- Is the person willing to listen without judgment?
- Does the person's maturity level justify the validity of their opinion?
- Is the person equipped to provide insight on the specific situation?
- Could self-interest be at the heart of their statements?

If their guidance passes through the filters, consider acting on it; if the filters leave no truth or credibility behind, move on.

Street-view mentors bypass these filters. We don't need to consider the source of their guidance, and we don't need to search for the truth. We just need to listen.

DON'T BE A GHOST

Most people we meet won't be street-view mentors for us;
that doesn't mean we can't help them to make their journey
smoother.

So many times, I've seen people cut others out of their lives
for different reasons. Sometimes, they don't agree with
their politics, so they stop talking to them. Other times, religion gets in the way of people maintaining good friendships.

I've been guilty of this with friends and family over the
years. As I have grown and matured, I've realized that usually when I desire to cut someone out, it's because I fear a
tough conversation that I need to have with them.

Anytime I have cut someone out of my life without having
the conversation, I've felt as if I've been held hostage by the
other person. Yes, they aren't physically in my life anymore,
but they consume my mind and spirit. They torment me
from afar without even knowing it.

Cutting people out is a cheap alternative for courageous conversations and effectively communicated boundaries.

If you want to cut someone out because they've hurt you or wronged you, make sure you're able to do it without a hateful or vindictive spirit. If you can't, it's not the other person you need to reconcile with, it's *you*.

Don't cut someone out of your life because you think, act, or live differently. Growth doesn't mean you have the right to abandon people. Who cares if you're on opposite sides of a political firestorm? Why break up a friendship due to differences in religious opinions?

We don't outgrow people. We simply grow differently.

If you feel as though the person you want to ghost doesn't deserve your forgiveness, I get it. There have been people who have hurt me on purpose, and I felt like they didn't deserve my forgiveness. So, if you won't do if for them, do it for yourself. As a mentor told me once, unforgiveness is like drinking poison and waiting for your enemy to die.

We often have a tendency to surround ourselves with people who all think, look, and vote the same way. That's not a *community*; it's a *cult*.

We don't necessarily have to change the opinions of

others. The goal is to create a dialogue. Approach them with enthusiastic discovery. Try to exchange ideas without anger, frustration, or intolerance at the forefront. By having a conversation, we might not *change* anyone; we might *understand* someone, and vice versa.

> ## TURN INSIGHT INTO ACTION
>
> Consider how you might be trying to impose your perspectives, political views, or religious convictions on others. What would happen if you stopped pushing and started loving? How would that impact your relationships? You have your journey; let them have theirs.

An old Buddhist philosophy is to "demonstrate your dharma," which means to live the things you want to teach. Jesus said it like this: "Do unto others what you would have them do to you." Ghandi echoed the same sentiment when he said, "Be the change you want to see in the world."

Approach with enthusiastic discovery, listen without judgement, and don't allow your mind to become consumed with conflict. Some translation of the Golden Rule shows up in every major religion.

NO MORE MR. NICE GUY

Let's say you meet a *nice* friend for lunch. As you both begin to enjoy the food, your nice friend notices a massive piece of spinach lodged between your front teeth and says...absolutely nothing.

The lunch concludes, and you've had a wonderful time with them because *nice* people are pleasant and complimentary. Unfortunately, your *nice* friend doesn't want to risk offending you to tell you something you need to hear. They care more about their comfort than they care about you.

At the end of the day when looking at yourself in the bathroom mirror, you realize how you have embarrassed yourself in every interaction over the last eight or so hours with a massive leafy green vegetable making an appearance every time you smiled.

Plato once said, "Your silence gives consent." By maintaining their silence in situations like that, nice people agree with your choices when they see you live in a way that could be harmful.

A *kind* person or a street-view mentor will react totally differently in that situation. As soon as they notice a bite of salad got left behind in your mouth, they'll tell you, "Hey, you've got a little something stuck right here," pointing to their own front teeth. That sort of reaction may make you uncomfortable or embarrassed for a minute or two, but it's much better to endure an awkward moment with your kind friend than suffer repeated embarrassment throughout the day and in some potentially key situations. Let's commit to being kind in our interactions with people and value those who are kind to us, even when it's uncomfortable.

PRIORITIZE GRATITUDE

Because the street-view mentors are the people closest to us, they're also the people we might take for granted. You might work a twelve-hour day, come home exhausted, and become short-tempered with the people you say you love the most. God knows, I've been guilty of this. Whenever possible, stop yourself before projecting your frustration leftover from the day's events on your street-view mentors. When you feel that urge beginning to overcome you, stop and give them a hug. Let them know that you're grateful for them. If we say we love them the most, let's treat them that way.

Be careful not to put obligations of your work above your own character. Likewise, make sure you don't value the relationships with friends over what your significant other needs from you.

Whether your street-view mentors are your wife, other family members, a long-time friend, coworkers, or a combination of all four, work to deepen those relationships. When you try to be everything to everybody, you end up being nothing to anybody, so let's make sure you take care of the people who matter most.

Street-view mentors are the people closest to you from a personal standpoint. In my case, my wife balances me. She is steady, detail-oriented, and analytical; I am none of those things. I'm sure if you look closely in your life, you'll find someone who counterbalances you in a similar way. This reminds me of a wonderful quote by Dale Carnegie: "If two partners always agree, one of them is unknot necessary."

Now that we've mentioned the people who are on the journey with you, let's take time to talk about the mentor who has a bit of a higher perspective and can help you navigate from a different place.

CHAPTER 9

THE WORLD-VIEW MENTOR

"Do what you love and work for whom you admire the most, and you've given yourself the best chance in life you can."

—WARREN BUFFET

At this point, you've read about the less conventional ideas of mentors, the ones that are overlooked and under-valued by most people. I think they are overlooked and undervalued by almost everybody. They're attitudes and perspectives, which is all you need to get started. Once you understand them and put them in action, you will attract the best traditional mentors, which I call the world-view mentor.

Many other books may provide you with a metaphorical treasure map to find your world-view mentor, as if they're in a secret underground bunker, waiting for you to ask them for their godly tutelage.

The truth is that no such treasure map or underground bunker exists. As cool as it would be to play Indiana Jones in your chase for mentorship, neither bullwhip nor wide-brimmed fedora is required to work with the world-view mentor.

You don't find the world-view mentor; they find you. Once you're doing the work, they'll take notice and want to help you. Your conversations with them will provide unique insight that you can turn into action to create breakthroughs in the real world.

ANSWERS AND QUESTIONS

A world-view mentor is like an A-10 Warthog military aircraft. Its primary purpose is to provide intel to ground troops. The plane flies over the environment, returns to the troops, and provides a report that outlines the location of enemy bunkers. With that information in hand, the ground troops can determine which path they'll take to get to their destination.

Another handy benefit of the A-10 is that it can flat-out eliminate enemy troops with a five-second barrage of gunfire. Occasionally, the A-10 will perform a low, slow flyover above an enemy camp as a way of saying, "Hey, I'm here! Don't *mess* with the troops, because I will end all of you."

Similar to the way an A-10 announces its presence, a world-view mentor can vouch for you. You get to borrow their credibility. If they recommend you for a job or promotion, that's their way of saying, "I endorse this person; I believe in them; I trust them." In that scenario, you get to borrow their reputation.

The world-view mentor has been to where you want to go. They have a knack for asking thoughtful questions before giving direct orders. This is helpful because it causes you to do your own problem-solving rather than executing a specific task without your own thoughts.

If you're not doing the work, good mentors won't notice you; they'll be too busy taking action of their own to spot somebody wandering around, looking for mentorship. They're not interested in pulling you across the finish line of your journey. Be wary of the supposed "mentor" who has enough free time to devote their energy to someone who hasn't earned the attention. There is a 99.9 percent probability they will do much more harm than good.

"BANKING" ON PEOPLE

My grandfather told me a story many years ago that
changed the way I see people. He said, "People treat each
other like banks, and banks have three kinds of customers:
bank robbers, transactional customers, and investors."

BANK ROBBERS

The first type of person walks into a bank and demands
money. They usually wear a mask that covers their entire
face except their eyes, point a gun at the teller, and say
something like, "Give me the money, and nobody gets
hurt!" We call these people bank robbers. With any luck,
they get caught and put in jail without anyone getting hurt.

Some people treat others like they're robbing a bank. A relationship with them is like a continuous circle of asking and
taking. They never invest anything into their relationships.
Be especially aware of these people and protect your energy
from them.

TRANSACTIONAL CUSTOMERS

The second type of person is a typical bank customer. They make consistent deposits while making an equal number of withdrawals. It's quid pro quo all the way in this transactional relationship.

This is the most typical example of a personal relationship. We'd certainly rather spend more time with this person than the bank robber. They don't stick out in any way because they take as much as they give, which is fine, not exceptional.

INVESTORS

The third type of person walks into a bank and makes one deposit after another. They rarely need to make a withdrawal because they build so much equity over the years that when they need resources, they live off the interest. These people invest consistently in others with no attachment to the timing of the outcome.

Over time, these people build so much personal equity that if they call us at 3:00 a.m. and ask us to bring a shovel and a trash bag to their house, we'll show up, with no questions asked.

This is the type of person with which my grandfather wanted me to develop and grow relationships.

Similar to how banking is a two-way street, so is a personal relationship. We have the choice to be one of those three types of people. Assuming we don't want to be bank robbers, we decide if we want to have ordinary, transactional relationships or if we want to build our relational equity and enjoy the benefits for a lifetime.

WORKING FOR FREE

One of the best investments we can make is giving our time to a world-view mentor. In a society where it's only a matter of time before we get charged for the air we breathe, consider the value of offering your time to a world-view mentor *for free* in exchange for the value it creates.

I worked for an outstanding world-view mentor—one of the best people I've ever known—for four years and never made a penny for those hours until later. I didn't make money immediately, but the investment I made changed the trajectory of my life. The value of the knowledge and skill I acquired during that time was priceless.

Think of it as if someone gave you the opportunity to attend a prestigious Ivy League school for free. The deal is that all you have to do is attend class and absorb the lessons. That's the gist of a college education anyway, and that's essentially what I did when I provided my services to Tom and Molly Breazeale for free over a four-year time period. The only difference was that after it was done, I didn't have hundreds of thousands of dollars in student loan debt. I had a priceless education.

I first met Tom Breazeale when times were tough for me. I had recently walked away from my family business. My wife had also just quit a great job in the energy industry to be a stay-at-home mom to our first child. In a thirty-day period, we lost 75 percent of our income and added a mouth to feed. To say the least, I was stressed, scared, and motivated to get out of the hole I was in.

With financial ruin weighing on my mind, I took an entry-level job as an outside sales rep for a national mattress manufacturer. One day, I received a call from my largest customer, who said, "I have a problem and I need you to get over here quickly."

When I went to see her, she said, "My boss wants me to take this stupid leadership course, and they want me to pick somebody to go with me. It's a three-hour course at night, and I'm not comfortable taking an employee. Would you go with me? It won't cost you anything."

At that time, *free* was exactly what I could afford, so I agreed to join her with zero apprehension. When we first sat down, the instructor—John Foust—said, "Hey, everybody, welcome to the Dale Carnegie program. We're excited to be here with you for the next *eight weeks.*"

"Wait, he said eight *hours*, right? No?" When it registered that he actually said *eight weeks*, I became overwhelmed and thought, "What the hell did I get myself into?"

Despite that initial panic, I am forever grateful that I stuck it out with that opportunity. That eight-week session, with John as my instructor and coach, fundamentally changed the trajectory of my life.

The Dale Carnegie program helped me develop the skills necessary to become a better communicator, presenter, businessperson, father, husband, and friend. There is not a single area of my life where that program has not had a massive impact. To this day, I consider that course to be divine intervention.

When the course was over, the instructor told everyone that if we wanted to become a graduate assistant, there was an opportunity to do so. We wouldn't get paid for the work. The benefit was in the experience we would receive by assisting one of the other instructors, who happened to Tom Breazeale. +Mark

I signed on for that opportunity as quickly as I could, because I was so impressed and excited about the material I had already learned. If this was going to be an extension of that, I figured, I'd be a fool *not* to get on board.

Being a grad assistant allowed me to build on the growth

I had in the program and develop a relationship with John and Tom.

The thing that was so impressive about Tom was that he really lived what he taught. He was the same person in front of the room as he was when no one was watching. He was the type of person I wanted to become.

And the icing on the cake was when I met his wife, Molly. When I met Molly, I knew Tom had hit a grand slam. I had the privilege to be a grad assistant for her a few times. The insight and coaching she provided left me feeling like I had just spent time with a certified saint.

I aspired to achieve what they had achieved in terms of character, integrity, and reputation. What attracted me most was who they were. They are great businesspeople, parents, friends, and, for me, the most important people (other than my wife) I've even known.

For the next four years, I worked nights and weekends. I took advantage of every chance to learn from Tom and Molly. They effectively became my surrogate parents and have had the largest impact in my life ever since. The skills I developed while working with them were invaluable.

If you have an opportunity for a similar situation, perhaps with an internship or apprenticeship somewhere, take it!

First, evaluate the potential impact of the person for whom you would be working. If you suspect that this person can teach you things you wouldn't be able to get anywhere else, you'd be a fool not to go for it. What do you have to lose? Time? At least give it a three-month trial period. At the end of that, if you feel like you're not getting enough value for your time, quit and move on to your next opportunity.

QUIT, BUT NEVER GIVE UP

As children, we're constantly told by loving and well-meaning adults to never quit. They want us to be resilient and fight through adversity. Here's a unique perspective: become great at *quitting*, just *never give up*.

Most often, quitting makes all the sense in the world, as long as we don't give up our search for other things we could be great at. Quit the things that don't work and where you can't excel. Quit the things that harm you, hurt you, limit you, and keep you from pursuing your purpose in life.

There's the difference between quitting and giving up. We should never give up our work toward continuous improvement in our career, relationships, and life. The best way to do that is to consistently quit the things that aren't for us.

If I didn't quit playing basketball at some point, I would be living under a bridge penniless right now. If I would have stayed in the furniture business, I would be miserable today. Similarly, if I hadn't quit that relationship in college, I wouldn't have married my greatest blessing, Merideth. The only way I ended up where I am today is because I quit all those other things that weren't for me. Every time we quit something that *isn't* for us, we open up space for the things that *are* for us.

I needed to quit all those things but not give up seeking continuous improvement. By doing that, I was able to meet Tom and Molly. I was also able to become a TEDx presenter and Dale Carnegie-certified instructor and coach. *Don't be afraid to quit, and never give up.*

HOW ABOUT A $500 CUP OF COFFEE?

While I was still working as an outside sales rep in 2011 (quitting some things but never giving up), I had the opportunity to talk with a man named Paul, whom I respected and admired a lot. Unfortunately, my approach wasn't the best. In hindsight, I would have handled this much differently. I feel it necessary to share with you so you don't make the same mistake.

I asked him if I could buy him a cup of coffee in exchange for his time to answer a few questions. His response was, "How much is that cup of coffee going to cost?" I was taken by surprise and replied, "What do you mean?" He said, "Do you have any idea how much my time is worth?" At that point, I had obviously insulted him, so I told him that I knew his time was worth much more than a three-dollar cup of coffee.

Luckily, he was gracious enough to meet with me despite my ignorance. I wouldn't recommend using that approach because it didn't seem appropriate.

Our interaction was short and sweet. Nonetheless, I received some solid mentorship. Paul first relayed his experience in the job market. He told me to never take a job before I was ready. He also said to make sure I'm consistently pissing off the right people. Both of these opinions came from real-world experience he had gained in his career. They weren't just things he read out of a textbook; he lived them.

Taking a job you're not ready for will almost always lead to poor results, which in turn will lead to wasted time and a negative experience.

Pissing off the right people is another way of standing up for what you believe in. If you live your life with integrity, it should irritate those who do not live with integrity. If you prioritize your family, it should annoy those who choose things over their loved ones.

Later on, I realized how grateful I was that he shared his

experience with me. It turns out listening to his experience was much more beneficial than providing advice on something he might not have known enough about. Experience over advice is an important distinction to make when working with anyone.

> **TURN INSIGHT INTO ACTION**
>
> If someone's time is worth $500 per hour, don't insult them by offering to buy them a cup of coffee for their time...unless the coffee comes with a check for $497. Instead, ask yourself how you might add value to them first.

EXPERIENCE OVER ADVICE

Julius Caesar is credited with saying, "Experience is the best teacher of all things." Centuries later, there's still a lot of truth to those words. Let's not misinterpret them to mean that we have to wait to experience everything ourselves. Experience is only the best teacher if we also learn from the experience of others.

Without a doubt, you can learn a lot from dealing with a hardship or correcting a mistake of your own. Wouldn't you prefer to learn the same lesson by reading a book or having a conversation with someone else?

You don't need to get punched in the teeth to learn not to tell the guy who looks like a professional MMA fighter that his haircut looks funny. Instead, listen to a story about someone who learned that lesson for you (and lived to tell about it). It's much less painful that way.

TURN INSIGHT INTO ACTION

When seeking mentorship, an essential rule to follow is to never ask for *advice*. Instead, ask them to share their *experience* with you.

If you ask someone for advice, they'll tell you what they think you should do in the unique situation with which you've presented them. The problem is that advice is a person's best guess; it's not always accurate to the current circumstance.

Even the people you respect most have never walked one foot in your shoes. If you share many of the same personality traits and thought processes, they still don't have your exact DNA. They may not know the best customized solution for you. They might even give advice that could blow up in your face.

When we ask for advice, we get a best guess; when we ask for experience, people typically tell us a story. Stories have infinite meaning and aren't based on conjecture.

If the person is willing to share something, they might ask why we're interested. That allows us to tell them what we're working towards, which could be an excellent way to strengthen the relationship. If we achieve success by leveraging their experience, we report back to them with gratitude about how well it worked. Mentors love to know they're having a positive impact.

Handle your relationships with mentors with care. Show gratitude and make sure your interactions with them aren't a nonstop series of asks. What I mean is, don't ask them for something every time you talk to them. They want to be treated as a human, like everybody else. They're not a mentor vending machine, where you put in the credits you've earned with them, push an appropriate button, and acquire amazing insight. If all of your interactions with them are asking for experience, access, or a favor, they won't want to continue their relationship with you. Relationships with a world-view mentor work best when the interactions are friendly, engaging, and valuable to both parties. Actually, relationships of any kind work best that way.

CONCLUSION

"You know, you do need mentors, but in the end, you really just need to believe in yourself."

–DIANA ROSS

Congratulations! You now have full awareness of the 5½ mentors that have always been there and can help you learn, grow, and develop from everyone and everything. Take a look at a quick summary of the big-picture lessons from each.

- **The Anti-Mentor (Half-Mentor)** – It can be hard to allow this person to teach us anything, but we have so much to learn from them. They can teach us invaluable lessons regarding patience, forgiveness, resilience, and much more; we have to stop avoiding them all the time and reframe our interactions with them to be more beneficial.

- **The Micro-Mentor** – You don't need permission or access to do something incredible. Live with enthusiastic discovery, and learn, grow, and develop from everyone and everything that is already around you.
- **The Digital Mentor** – You have been empowered with the greatest resource in the history of humankind! How will you use it?
- **The Categorical Mentor** – Nobody's perfect. Take the best lessons that everybody has to offer and chisel away the things that will not serve you well. Start sculpting your masterpiece today.
- **The Street-View Mentor** – If you're about to do something *really* stupid, these are the people who know, love, and care about you enough to tell you about it. Listen carefully, because these people have earned the right to have a strong voice in your life.
- **The World-View Mentor** – Good mentors in the more traditional sense will find you when you're already doing the work. By engaging in similar behaviors, this person will *want* to help you. Remember to show gratitude and appreciate their generosity. Tell them when something they shared with you works well.

ACTION REVEALS ANSWERS

If you desire to honor yourself and the life you've been given, keep in mind the advice my good friend Mark Kinsley always reminds me of: *action reveals answers*. What does it mean? If applied knowledge is powerful (and it is), use your newfound awareness of the 5½ mentors to apply, test, iterate, and fail. Then, do it again, again, and again. Give yourself the freedom to fail. After all, failure is how you learn the most.

Along the journey of our attempts at taking action, we should ask questions, try new things, show up differently, observe our outcomes, and adjust accordingly.

GOOD NEWS/BAD NEWS

There's good news and bad news that comes with finishing this book. The bad news is that nobody is coming to save you. I mentioned in the Introduction that my Yoda never showed up, and yours probably won't either. It doesn't matter if you're waiting for Yoda, the A-Team, or the genie from *Aladdin* to show up; none of them is coming to save the day, grant you three wishes, or mold you into a superhero.

The good news is that nothing is stopping you. Mentorship is not a gift that is given to you. Mentorship is a gift you give yourself with the help of everyone and everything.

ABOUT THE AUTHOR

DOUG STEWART is a TEDx speaker, certified Dale Carnegie Instructor, performance coach, and mentorship thought leader. He is known for utilizing original and adaptive methods to help people pursue a life of purpose through enthusiastic discovery. Most importantly, Doug is a devoted husband to his best friend, Merideth, and proud father to his children, Kendall and Kendrick. For more information, visit DougStewart919.com.

Made in the USA
Coppell, TX
23 November 2020